my tap root

Volume II

Poems
by
Jennie Rose

Azalea Art Press
Sonoma | California

© Jennie Rose, 2023.
All Rights Reserved.

ISBN: 978-1-943471-69-0

Cover Design
by Karen Mireau

I Dedicate This Book:

To myself and my extraordinary survival skills,
probably inherited in my DNA from my father
who survived The Fall of Corregidor,
The Bataan Death March and four years of slavery
in the iron mines as a Japanese Prisoner of War

My uncompromising principles

My learned ability to recognize when I am wrong,
to apologize, make amends, and not to do
whatever it was again

My struggle to survive years of poor health, cancer,
and numerous surgeries, with an overall attitude of positivity
and gratitude for all those who showed up
along the way to help me

My belief in a Loving God
and the Power of Prayer

My difficult, painful, and disciplined evaluations
of relationships, and choices to end those that were toxic
and nourish those that are nurturing

My devotion to self-improvement
and ongoing education, learning, and living in reality
and truth in the here and now

My finishing what I start

My commitment to myself to live
free of Codependence and help those
who need me along Life's Way

I also dedicate this book
to my readers in the hope that these poems
will provide guidance and light on your path

Other Books
by Jennie Rose

My Tap Root
Volume I
Azalea Art Press
2016

CONTENTS

Introduction
by Karen Mireau

Poems

2022

Grounded	2
April 16	3
Surprise Sociopath Attack	7
Betrayals	9
Clouds of Fear	10
Thoughts of Change	12
My Fountain	13
Putin's War	14
Community Outrage: Defiant Sociopath	15
Where is Soul?	17
In Response to Where is Soul	19
My Father's Obituary	21
Growth and God	22
My Thinking Cap	24
My Beloved Alex	25
Oh Ching!	27
Space	28
Ending Relationships and Marking Them Closed	31
Christmas Eve 2022	33
Tulips and Hypo Arousal	35
When	37

2021

My Story	39
Waiting with Courage	40
I'm in Mourning	41
Days of Infamy	42
Things Are Different	43
Christmas Day	44
Christmas 2021	45
Slaves of Obsession	46
Lost Christmas	47
New Year's 2021	49
Turning the Calendar's Page	50
Backyard	51
Turning Seventy-four October 22, 2021	52
Seventy-four Years Young	53
To Be the Me My Dog Loves	54
Oh Jolie! Please Wait for Me at the Rainbow Bridge	55
Gifts and Betrayal	57
Mean and Hateful	60
Confused Aging	61
A Friend That Wasn't Really a Friend	62
My Inner Child	64
Free From the Fourth Commandment	65
Re'my Turning Three	68
Today to Therapy Came God	69
Lies from my Mother	70
A Crisis Addict	Compulsive Caretaker	73
Outgrowing Relationships	Losing Friends	75

2020

The King Wears No Clothes	78
I'm Afraid for My Country	80
I'm in Fear	81
Trump's a Criminal and a Loser	82
Lies	83
Racism—Newly Old in 2020	84
Our World Has Changed	86
Little Truffles Girl (A Poem with Tears)	88
Betrayal 2020	90
Hope	91
Your History and the High Road	93
Thoughts	94
Chains	95
Crises and Friends	96
Acceptance	97

2019

When Trauma Reigned	99
Quiet	101
Pursuit of Honor	102
I'm So Sorry	103
When the Time Comes	105

2018

Grieving to Peace	107
Time to Say Goodbye to My Beloved Boy	110
Six Months Old Today	112

Beneath the Snow . . .
    Beyond the Storm   113
Camus   114
My Grief is Less Today   115
Why Now?   117
Gratitude   119
I Sat in the Garden   120
Collapse of Grief   121
I Choose   125
I Love and Loved You
    My Brother   126
The Cost of Change   127
STOP   128
My Tiny Warrior   129

2017

Today's the Day
    My Best Friend Died   133
How Tall You Stand   134
And I Wonder
    Where You Are Now?   135
Ashgebat Turkmenistan   136
Today   138
What Comes in Silence?   139
The In-Between   141
I am Precious—It is So   144
On the Other Side
    of Forgiveness   146
Trees   148
Death   149
Bereaved   151
Poetry   152

2016

Trauma Reaction	154
Blame and Relationships	156
Circling the Wagons	158
Strays	159
Teachers, Competence and Humility	161
Clarity	163
Consequences of Texting	165
New Ways	167
Controlling Me	170
Children	172
Old Soldiers Sing	174
Shadows of Shame	176
Belonging to Myself	178
Consequences of Choices— The Price We Pay	180
The Journey	182
Who is That?	184
Cement Tracks	186
Healthy Aging	188
Ending Old and Broken Relationships	190
Solutions and Problems	193
Limitless the Clouds, the Sky	195
Time	197
Being	199
Departure	201
Truth With Honor	203
Imagining the Future	205
Absent Pets	207
Clear Sight	208
Grace	210
Exhausted	211

The Power and the I of NO	214
Lap Dogs and Thoughts	217
True Story	219
Black Panther	222
Life and Moving Forward	224

2015

My Story	227
Easter Comes On Wings of Song	228
Faith Mountain	230
A Balanced Legacy	232
Less is More	234

2014

Choices and Consequences	236
Rules of Life	237
Forgiveness for My Dad	238
Fog	242
10:00 a.m.	243
The Glue of Friendship	245
Sociopaths	248
Filaments	249

2013

Night Dreams	251

2012
    Birthdays   253
    Finding Balance   255
    Camus and Reiki   256
    Gently Offer Empathy   257
    I am Me   259
    My Journey   262

2010
    Relationships   266

Acknowledgments   *268*

Resources   *275*

About the Author   *287*

Contact | Book Orders   *288*

Introduction

The poems of Jennie Rose are an extraordinary alchemical mix of truth and dare—a crash course in trauma therapy that exceeds any of our preconceived notions. Line by line, poem by poem, she shows us a direct path to discovering our "tap root" and how to establish a deep-rooted sense of Self.

Her work is rather like a literary *tarot*. Pick any poem, any page, and you will find an answer to the questions that plague you, or at the very least a trailhead that will lead you wherever you need to go.

Jennie has counseled those in crisis for well over a decade. As a therapist, she knows intimately the sources of our shame, our silenced wounds, our betrayals and psychic injuries, our inherent resistance to change—including her own.

Jennie's first full-length collection of poems, *My Tap Root*, spanned the years of 2009 to 2015. Her new work comprises unpublished poems from 2010 to 2023.

They are presented in reverse chronological order to better emphasize her journey of being diagnosed with breast cancer, suffering through multiple surgeries, as well as her experiences of painful and personal losses along the way.

Her recovery in 2022 is one that resonates as a universal testament to healing, both physically and spiritually, and as an enduring inspiration to anyone who is searching for a way to become more grounded.

—Karen Mireau
May, 2023

2022

Grounded

I'm now grounded with a Tap Root
I'm secure with roots intact
Spreading roots are intertwining
Life enriching, solid fact—

Not enmeshed, yet all connected
Each does nourish one and all
Roots are boundaried, independent
Steady, sturdy, strong and tall

Deep in color, vibrant, pulsing
There is life day after day
Seasons pass to stormy weather
Growth continues, tree does sway

In the strong winds and the hail storms
In the drought and in the sun
Tree and roots are ever living
Grounded Tap Root—'til life's done

April 16

I've childlike curiosity
I've become a different me
I can't believe who I am now
Different creativity

I don't do what I used to do
In ways both big and small
I sometimes peer into the glass
And marvel at it all

It seems just yesterday when I
Was stressed, tied up in knots
I do not recognize myself
Without my *shoulds* and *oughts*

Things now seem so straightforward that
I ask question: "Where's my Fear?"
Surrounded me with tendrils fast
For lo these many years

It's absence such a stark contrast
To how I've lived my life
Not missed . . . and yet so very strange
Absent trauma, drama, strife

I feel I'm wearing all new clothes
My face looks less worn, aged
My eyes are youthful, eager, bright
My mind fully engaged

Life's full and rich . . . less busy now
My activities unchanged
'Tis me that's different . . . inside/out
As if all's been rearranged

Feelings of Gratitude abound
Much accomplished every day
The flow . . . it's just not what it was
Thank you sprinkles what I say

The little bumps that come along
Resolution . . . instantly
No fuss and feathers! No more spin!
No drain on my energy

The consequences crystal clear
Of the choices I do make
It's easier to change my mind
Mid-stream check . . . new course I take

I'm getting used to this new state
Before was disadvantaged
Live moderation. Stay the course
No longer live unmanaged

Improvements come most every week
Active practice: Gratitude
I focus on the positives
And kindness. I'm not rude

Sarcasm no longer choice
Nor judgment, fault or blame
Responsibility's the key
It's become my middle name

My speaking, listening have changed
Connections with good clarity
The puzzle does arrange itself
And is very clear to me

Confusion from the Past is gone
With my codependent fog
Trauma repetition patterns
Are now not entered in my log

The freedoms present deep within
Are hard to articulate
And every day I wake up with
Fresh and new . . . an unmarked slate!

Responsibility is mine
Moderation as LifeStyle
This takes some getting used to . . . and
Walking High Road is worthwhile

Recovery's the beginning
There is so much more. There's fun!
Neurofeedback's gift to me was
Thunderstorms morphed into sun

So Gratitude and Daily Prayers
Are plentiful every day
And I respond with choices wise
To what Life brings me today

I've helped my own PTSD
My brain's become resilient
Trauma patterns now replaced with
Cognitions sometimes brilliant

Surprise myself and others too
Who knew this could be real?
Inherent and best gift of all
Crystal clear on what I feel

Surprise Sociopath Attack

When my NO is disrespected
Disrespect yells loud . . . unheard
Overt gesture of false kindness
Hides agenda for "Last Word"

Blindsided. Unexpected
I was vulnerable, off guard
So purposeful, deliberate
Hit me very, very hard

Almost missed it in the playing
Of a game so very old
She had learned it from her mother
Became blatant and so bold

She would NOT hear another's NO
No matter subject, time or place
Had her own concepts, agenda
Intent to force to win this race

I will not tolerate such disrespect
ANY/ALL will hear my NO
And if they can't . . . I'm done with them
No second chances! NO!

I know I speak with clarity
Misunderstandings don't occur
So Malice here's deliberate
Not to listen or concur

Won't wait around for her to learn
Not my job to care or tell
She chose to wreck relationship
Copied Mother–taught her well

Betrayals

My heart hurts at the betrayals
Surrounding me on every side
People I thought I could trust
Hard to "see" how they have lied

Not been honest or transparent
In their selfishness and greed
It's appalling! I am wounded
They won't listen . . . They won't heed

Few do care for one another
Discarded that so long ago
Now entitled and Me First
Not for others. They're no show

Tap delete and move ahead
Piled them like rocks at side of road
No looking back . . . what might have been
No sense to carry heavy load

That is not mine. Were my beliefs
Misplaced in others? Deep the grief!
Few now do walk with me today
In gratitude for them I pray

Clouds of Fear

Now the clouds of fear have vanished
View obscured by fog is clear
Sun so bright brings tears to my eyes
Shadows, smoke in rear view mirror

Clarity is now astounding
Explanations now bright white
In the wound that's always waiting
Truth resounds with healing light

Blame, fault, judgment do dissolve
No longer found within, without
I own my part and I change me
Responsibility not doubt

In freedom there is firm resolve
Pulsing rainbow. Dim the Past
Recovery includes relapse
Step by Step will bind it fast

I'm different, growing every day
Emerging into wondrous me
Please be my partner on this path
Steady when I slip, don't see

Pitfalls and quicksand on the way
Give me patience and your hand
Destination unclear within
This inner landscape's land

With time the dust will settle soft
Obscuring path behind
And losing fear I finally gain
Crisp clarity of mind

Thoughts of Change

I'm purposeful, deliberate
Not spinning round and round
Decisions are now well thought out
A mess no longer found

Was so long due to my distress
Confusion did abound
And where I walked the weeds did grow
Constant clean-up I sure found

No vision clear
No choices wise
I kept stumbling on and on . . .

My Fountain

My fountain sings a lovely song
It splashes down and o'er
So similar yet always new
It mutes the traffic's roar

It's levels three. The basin's deep
The pump works day and night
In rain or shine it sings its song
Its song so brave . . . so bright

It's peaceful at the water's edge
The splashing, soothing sound
My garden is my refuge safe
Fence, plants and trees surround

The sound of water carries us
To lands so far away
The dappled sunlight sparkles there
Dreams dance in fountain's spray

Putin's War

We're going off to war again
And Putin leads the charge
His tanks, troops surround poor Ukraine
His ego is so large

He wants its natural resources
Its oil and its gas
He doesn't care for people's lives
Destroyed when he does pass

It's only that he wants his way
This temper tantrum child
A Psychopath who's just like Trump
Who cheers him on with Ego wild

No Conscience sees no consequence
Of lives disrupted, lost
Resulting trauma heaves new load
On what's there from the past

And people crushed by just too much
Don't flourish . . . wither, die
Putin wreaks havoc every day
And tells the world his lies

Community Outrage: Defiant Sociopath

Community was outraged when
He would not apologize
Would not submit himself for treatment
Refused to be "cut down to size"

Refused admitting he was human
Flawed, imperfect like the rest
In frank Denial and Delusion
Still considered he was best

Of what? Or Who? It doesn't matter
His actions did betray us all
He would not show to pay the piper
And he did disregard his fall

From the Grace he "did believe in"
He sure did preach it from his throne
When it came time for him to get some
He ran away to be alone

It is sad to see betrayal
Thus the high and mighty crack
When there's repentance, then forgiveness
Instead, Sociopath attacks

And rejects his need for treatment
Perhaps he knows there is no cure
For someone born without a conscience
Has no space to be unsure

He needs to lord it over others
And always be the one in charge
He is a taker, not a giver
And poses risk to world at large

He is a fraud who has no feelings
Although in form he looks a man
And so he'll hurt you without blinking
He's so good at it that he can

So run away now. Don't get closer
You cannot help him. Stay away!
You'll become another victim
If you believe what he does say

Block your ears! Don't look in his eyes!
Flat and hard. There's no one home
Smile is false and ever shallow
Run away! Let him alone

Leave him be to his Creator
God alone can help him when
He does die and face his Master
Consequences there and then

Where is Soul?

I was not afraid of aging
Until covid came to stay
Blockaded all my avenues
And I can't run away

It's Everywhere. In every land
It's expensive now to die
I am bored with doing nothing
Airports scrambled. Planes don't fly

People desperate to be normal
Act instead as desperate fools
Common sense goes out the window
Media lies are major tools

And the problem spreads like cancer
Hidden cells found everywhere
And the litter spreads like pollen
Deep crevices. No sun's glare

There's no purpose. There's no reason.
All's amok in Chaos' rage
There's no path 'cept swirling darkness
End of dark is tight barred cage

The crowd surges ever onwards
Without destination, plan or thought
And the corpses flatten gullies
To a plain of *Should* and *Ought*

Faceless future. Barren landscape.
All is same with shriveled soul
I stop running. There is silence.
Nothing left. There is no goal

*(please see the following response to this poem
written by Quincy Garfield)*

In Response to Where is Soul?
by Quincy Garfield

I thought about your question,
Where is soul?
And read your beautiful phrasing
Each line descriptively amazing.

Your gift of expressing feelings
Is powerful and strong
The darkness to your language reads
Like a very sad song

But despite the virus
And all its woes
My spirit sees hopefulness
Wherever it goes.

Glass half full
Or naturally positive of mind
I'm bolstered by efforts
I see of folks being kind

And yes, the nut jobs
Are fully employed in their madness
I resist the temptation
To get sucked up in their badness

Instead, I look out my window
I walk in the woods
And ignore the oughts
And the shoulds

I'm happy enough
To be upright and walking
Ignoring for now
The political squawking

I'm grateful for my family
And my dearest friends, too
And writing this poem
Just for you!

My Father's Obituary

Why did I know it was missing my name?
Just a gut feeling inside
Thrown out of my house in '81
Caught abusing me, he couldn't hide

Dissociated to black hole
His shit thrown to the street
I had no memory . . . no recall
So, not again did we meet

I spent my life in fear of this man
Relationships poisoned and bleak
Most of my nights I could not sleep
Was sometimes unable to speak

Now that he's dead I thought I was free
But he had rewritten his life
Edited out great ugly Truths
So charming he was with fourth wife

So I can rewrite my own story
Claim Vern as father beloved
At age twenty-five he came into my life
He loved ME! Daughter discovered

I changed my name to become Rose
To honor new father right here
I think he knows this in heaven
He always was there for me . . . Cheered!

Growth and God

I choose to have a busy life
With time to be alone
I don't like the computer much
I'd rather use the phone

Spend time with those who are aware
Of lifelong needs to grow
And change. Look deep within one's self
Or else it's all a show

Some I know don't want to change
They're happy with the Past
Live lives repeating old mistakes
And OH! they run so fast

Keeping up with this and that
No time to look inside
Their busyness is just a front
They're really trying to hide

The pain and anguish that they feel
From pain that they have caused
Or from the old Pain given to them
It's really up to God

To sort it out for all of us
He gives support and lessons
It's up to us to learn and grow
So we don't get more sessions

He gives us little ones to start
We ignore them at our cost
Then bigger ones He sends us next
Severe the pain. We're lost

And me, I like the little ones
He's used a train before
To help me pay attention when
He closes, opens doors

So now I work with those I meet
Who want to change and grow
I read and learn and practice
So I'm ready for His show!

My Thinking Cap

My thinking has been rearranged
From Why to just Acceptance
Feels unfamiliar. Still quite new
I have not learned the dance

Why some folks just cannot answer
It is simply what they do
In situations yet untried
Old patterns still are new

Yet tried again and yet once more
To see if they will work
Old habits are so hard to break
Yes! Even if they hurt!

New information found in books
CDs and therapy
Will change, re-pattern tired old ways
New thinking sets me free

My Beloved Alex

It's quiet where you used to be
All still when I come home
It's taken me a good long while
To really be alone

I wish I could turn back the clock
And quiet all your fears
Of getting old and going blind
I cannot stop Time's years

They march right on and take me too
If I say Yes or No
They trip me up and knock me down
Keep moving fast and slow

I miss the times I talked to you
About my life, my days
You listened ever patiently
And then you had your say

If I was late in coming home
Your comments at the ready
I miss the way you welcomed me
Saying, "Steady, Ellie, steady."

It's quiet where you used to be
With thoughts of you I cry
I understand you can't be here
So hard to say goodbye

I'd like it if you'd watch for me
So I won't be alone
In heaven where your sight is clear
And, finally, we'll be home

Oh Ching!

Oh Ching! My friend I miss you so
And so often I get sad
And wish that you'd come back again
And make me oh so glad!

I miss the ways you curled to sleep
And opened, closed your eyes
I'd find you where you shouldn't be
And you'd act so surprised!

It wasn't time to say goodbye!
At least for me that's true
I hope you're somewhere soft and warm
That's purrrfect! Just for you

In memory you'll always be
My Special one! My Ching!
Please wait for me beside the gate
When Heaven's bells do ring

And show me where to walk and play
In sunshine bright and warm
And sit and tell me how you've been
While curled up in my arms

Space

Pictures framed, selected groupings
What's the theme that ties them tight?
Are they scattered without pattern?
Represent my inner sight?

Have I taken time to learn just
Who I am in outward guise
What reflects my inner turmoil
Jumbled, tumbled, wisdom, wise?

Have I learned that my surroundings
Clearly mirror who I am?
How I live in space created
Speaks out loud! Doors open . . . slam

If my space won't let me dance in
Free abandon spin and twirl
What constraints do hold me back as
When I was just a little girl?

Time to sift and sort, be ruthless
What in here is really me?
How have I collected baggage
Filling needs I couldn't see

As holes in Self that need attention
Their repair my job alone
I am worth the time and effort
Transform chaos into home

Home where I can see who I am
Reflected in my use of space
And decorated with deep peace
Seen and felt in body, face

I will part with past collections
If they don't reflect me now
I'll need help to do this sorting
Serene support to show me how

Because my outer life's my inner
Not integrated yet to whole
Separate parts that need connecting
Into cohesive, grounded soul

Each of us comes to this moment
Scattered parts and pieces wild
We need help with concentration
Integrating Precious Child

Disorganized? Perfectionist?
How we live shows who we are
We can create cohesive whole
Serenity's right here . . . not far

Discipline? It is required
Some needed choices will cause pain
Without it there's no freedom, space
Cocoon to butterfly again

So, if your past now blocks your present
It's time to pause, create a dream
Eliminate what's in your way
New colors, patterns create scheme

That's yours in all of who you are
Reflecting who you are today
It's time to focus, tackle this
It's time you did your life your way

Ending Relationships and Marking Them Closed

Can't be in a relationship
Not nourishing to me
It is toxic and unhealthy
Without good energy

It's not growing, not expanding
No new fuel! No new glue!
It's contracting, losing borders
You are different now. Me too

You are still a Codependent
Childish, refuse to grow
Into a competent adult
Take charge of you, your life, your show

I don't like me when I'm with you
Triggered into childish rage
By your delusions, fantasy
It's time to go. I'll turn the page

Need relationship that HEARS me
Don't need one that cannot
We will go our separate ways now
Need to grow. Not stay and rot.

I will love you for our memories
From the Past! They were quite grand
No new glue to take their place now
I'll move on in adult land

Where Reality is king! And
Codependence has no place
I will pray as I am passing
Asking God to give you Grace

Christmas Eve 2022

There's nothing wrong with Christmas
So there's something wrong with me
Don't want to decorate, do cards
Or put up a Christmas tree

Don't want to get the boxes out
Of ornaments through the years
Too many of them sad and dark
It won't allay my fears

Don't feel the Joy of Season bright
I prefer to be alone
Sometimes don't even want to talk
So I don't answer the phone

There is no good/bad reason why
It is just the way it is
I've been quite ill the whole year long
I'm flat inside. No fizz

Just sit and read and cuddle dog
And I drink cups of hot tea
I wait for Christ to come again
On this night, on Christmas Eve

He's the reason for this season
Not for all the shops and sales
But He gets lost in bustling crowds
It is way beyond the pale

Today, this Eve, it's time for Church
Music, sermon and to pray
For Hope and Joy to please return
And bless my Christmas Day

With gratitude I say to God
I've lived another year
I thank You for each special day
For my smiles and my tears

And ask if I can have more time
To LIVE and LISTEN, PRAY
To live with Joy within my heart
'Til next year's Christmas Day

Tulips and Hypo Arousal

I'm crawling out of my cocoon
A process slow with fear
Of what I might encounter there
Skies blue, not gray, and clear?

I didn't know I was cocooned
Tight banded, void inside
Clueless of light and the exit
Safer to stay warm and hide

Cold's a big sign of this problem
Four jackets where others wear one
Hat, gloves and scarf in the doorway
Ten, twenty minutes I'm done

Can't write poetry, make a list
Or organize things that I need
My brain full of chaos yet quiet
Moving half of my usual speed

Conversation's not great – mostly flat
Can't recall what I've read or said
Memory's holes keep on growing
Unsure if I'm living or dead

This is called Hypo Arousal
Comes straight from my PTSD
When I'm overwhelmed or too tired
Dissociation saves me

Puts wall between me and trauma
So I don't disintegrate
But then comes black hole or cocoon
Numb, clueless I hide at the gate

I don't know I'm there and need help
Cannot ask others for a hand
I do not have words or courage
Or awareness I'm in foreign land

So it's quiet, long hours of sleeping
Not eating or doing self care
Just getting thru days and the nights
Not questioning that I am WHERE?

And suddenly, pinpoint of light
Pierces gloom of cocoon
And I start to peel back the layers
Find SELF in familiar room

And again the process begins
Re-enter the world as it is
Help from Greg eases my way
When he takes my hand in his

Slowly I return to normal
My Window of Tolerance clear
Not hypo or hyper but present
Tulips bloom, eaten by deer

When

When the guns stop roaring
When deadly bullets cease
When the tanks turn rust to dust
Then there will be Peace

When War is not the answer
Nor Greed the driving force
When Ego's chains tight fastened
World can set a different course

When Pride removes his armor
And as equal sits to talk
When to really hear and listen
Is as common as a walk

Then there's Hope for generations
Those who've been and yet to be
Less the turmoil and the trauma
Future will be bright! You'll see

2021

My Story

Now it's time to write my story
What is best for me to say?
How can I explain my journey
Philosophy of Day By Day?

Most of it is way beyond me
Why that focus? Why that choice?
Truly I do not have answers
Poetry did give me voice

Voice? the usual way of talking
Telling others what you think
And feel, believe and understand
Verbal skating on ice rink

With pirouettes and jumps, fast turns
Patterns elegant, sublime
To music heard by only you
Few others hear the rhythm, rhyme

And you connect in conversation
Oh the joy of being heard!
A taste of heaven here on earth
Conversation's music? . . . Words

So today I write my story
It is what it is for now
More will happen. It's not over
I'm in charge of me. So Wow!

Waiting With Courage

The waiting is the hardest when
You don't know all the facts
When there's really nothing you can do
Until the time does come to act

When your mind is full of questions
And your heart is full of fear
And you can't make something happen
Not in charge! Your way not clear

It's time to pray and ask for help
Let Go of all control
Be quiet deep within yourself
Communicate with heart and soul

Past tests and consultation
And moving forward you engage
Your life and situation
Small, like pawn, upon Life's stage

I'm in Mourning

I'm in mourning for Liz Cheney
For the party that I knew
For the lies it manufactures
And its' statements so untrue

I'm in fear and trepidation
For the country of my heart
For denial, obfuscation
Blatant falsehoods. Lies from start

Meant confusion and acceptance
Of alternative reality
To those on steady diet
Of false news from their TV

Bigger tragedy forthcoming
This is front end of the wave
Brings fear, disintegration
Of what many tried to save

But there is Evil now abiding
In the Land of Home and Free
And mass silence and oppression
Of what they don't want to see

Our Freedom's fragile . . . fraying fast
Lies continue, rolling on
Liz Cheney stood almost alone
Midst the lies. They're never gone

Days of Infamy

Infamy again is with us
Eighty years. It's close and deep
Now the enemy's amongst us
On many pathways it does creep

Shadowed and wrapped in stripes and stars
Face unclear. Eyes bleak and blind
Loud raucous voices shout the lies
Some escalate, respond in kind

And still the covid cases rise
Hospitals fill in every land
Workers drained . . . PTSD
Chaos, infamy hand in hand

Things Are Different

Things are different. Things are changing
Time is passing, moving on
While I'm watching I am changing
Other changes seem so wrong

Why restrict the voting choices
Limit hours, boxes, days?
Supreme Court voted it okay
This is now. Was not always

Hate and violence seem the norm now
From both old and young alike
Germinating under black rocks
Old the pattern. New the strike

Hate is passed along through families
No one ever knows the source
Always been there. Newly nurtured
Has become a normal course

Doesn't need a rhyme or reason
So easy to rise up again
It's that Other . . . no one sees him
'Til scapegoat needed. Shout Amen

Christmas Day

First year of present decade ends
In turmoil, death and strife
Harmony and common sense have
Almost vanished from my life

My circle of friends is shrinking
Some have lost their place, their chair
High intensity politics
Have no room when I am there

It's too exhausting to keep up
Folks do not police their speech
They talk so loud and think so small
Harmony so out of reach

It's not confined to just my land
Growing everywhere on earth
Acid engraved in DNA
Destabilizes folks' net worth

Folks rushed in a hurry don't see
They miss the pitfalls and the thorns
No critical thinking is used
No discernment. I'm sad, forlorn

And I pray for Peace and for Love
For a world spiraling down
Hope for hearing sharp and eyes
Bright joy and laughter, singing sounds

Christmas 2021

I had a tough time with Christmas
In past years that wasn't so true
Sickness is very depressing
Depleting, defining and blue

Smile forced. My greetings were shallow
Making plans didn't turn out so well
Always tired and not quite all there
And way too much silence was hell

I still have a huge bag of mail
It darkens my table with dread
I'm jealous of what others did
I sat in my house. Warm packs. Meds

I can't believe I'm so tired
Exhausted and worn out and in
Activities few. My pace is slow
Wondering when I will win

Slaves of Obsession

Unvaccinated I salute
Your stupid lies and selfishness!
Entitled to the deaths you choose
Responsible for country's mess

Drink deep perverse lies from "The Twelve"
Top disinformation sources
Cause new pandemic from the old
Cause country to reverse its course

YOU! You murder squad of millions
Lack Conscience, Truth, Integrity
Blind, deaf like lemmings leap the cliff
To rush to page of history

You won't be here for next election
You'll fill the ground with graves
I've no pity or compassion
You chose to act like slaves

Lost Christmas

Covid new arrived and stronger
Comes to trample plans, stoke fears
Victims everywhere increasing
Dark horizons. Many tears

Unvaccinated fill the rooms
Pushing limits, overflow
Staff exhausted without surcease
Anti-vaxxers still say NO

Borders closed and shops are shuttered
Christmas market stalls are dark
Stay close to home and wear your mask
Carefully walk dog in the park

Nearly two years since it started
Changed the world so many ways
Travel industry is broken
Bankruptcies coming. Soon the day

And the selfish keep on spreading
Virus as if it did not count
They're responsible for deaths and
Increasing cases as they mount

The world has changed and people in it
ME! ME! ME! so loud the chant
To hell with you or any other
As they riot, rave and rant

I am sad to miss my journey
With my friend of many years
But her health to me too precious
So I'm drying all my tears

New Year's 2021

As I wait and watch it coming
Hour by hour drawing near
Round the world are celebrations
Welcoming a brand New Year

Moving forward . . . what's the same?
What will we find different, new?
Experiences that we choose
Provide direction . . . me and you

Turning the Calendar's Page

And I turn the calendar's page
New possibilities wait
No need for a re-run of Past
Path ahead has wide open gate

'Tis I who must take the first step
Into a brand new tomorrow
Head high and my eyes straight ahead
Dropping my burdens and sorrow

Good memories float in my space
I'm part of the Present, the Now
My Journey! what really matters
As I learn new ways, why and how

Backyard

I'm generous with money
Not so generous with time
I hold back much more than before
Avoiding slips and slime

I'm much more cautious now than then
I walk instead of run
Some is age and some is learned
I gravitate to sun

Prefer it dappled, not too bright
And shadowed, hidden spaces
For birds to hide and build their nests
Or flowers showcase faces

The feeder feeds. It's squirrel proof now
Suet feeder hangs near-by
A dozen species stop to snack
Or drink or sing or fly

Turning Seventy-four
October 22, 2021

What a birthday! Seventy-four!
Calls, balloons, and flowers, cards
Pizza dinner made by Cassie
Perfect day. Idyllic yard.

Emails, books, hat, wine from Donna
Bichon Pjs – like counting sheep
Creative Life Book with its card
And fourteen hours of passed-out sleep

Maribeth had drained the river
Shattered damn that held the pain
And delusion, deep depression
Sleeping . . . I did heal again

Didn't know my heart was hurting
I had walled it off for years
Drained the poison. Filled with Life Force!
Laughing, letting-go the tears

Now rebalanced, I'll move forward
Thanking God for Life and Friends
Feeling lighter. Heart expanding
Full of Joy and on the mend

(Please see the following poem in response by Quincy Garfield)

Seventy-four Years Young
By Quincy Garfield

Thanks for sharing your heart-felt words
Words with the wings of emotional birds

Flights of healing from sources of pain
Over the horizon of no more blame

In to the light of friends' enduring love
Landing softly on the beams above

Looking out with quiet joy
Of appreciating the warmth of this day's sun

Seventy-four years young and still full of fun!
Traveling on to one hundred and one!

To Be the Me My Dog Loves

Camus, I'm still caught by your picture
With your brown eyes so soft, serene
A heart full of love, compassion
For a world that to you wasn't mean

I miss you my beloved boy
Your love and dedication
I wandered far. You brought me home
In your eyes to see my reflection

My goal was too hard to achieve
Preferred to be through and through
The woman you saw with your eyes
Compassionate, loving like you

I'm still working on that ideal
Re'my nudges me into line
I pray and try hard every day
Need to be more like you to be fine

Oh Jolie!
Please Wait for Me at The Rainbow Bridge

Oh Jolie! My heart is breaking
Tears cascade down my face
You've been gone for nearly two years
And there's none to take your place

I gaze into your picture with
Background of orange and red
You're bright, alert and sitting -up
"Let's walk right now you said!"

I hold another photo with
Background of softest gold
Your sweet brown eyes are closing
Your soul slips out of my hold

And you're gone and I am screaming
Little Re'my's scared! Stop!
Start. So I hold you two together
Kissing, petting both to heart

And he kisses you to wake up
Once again and come to play
As I talk and reassure him
That he's the one who's going to stay

We called Joyce to come to see us
So that she could say goodbye
Bonnie came with tea and camera
Bringing love and hugs—sad cries

Rescued you at seven months
Blessed by you for thirteen years
Please wait by the Rainbow Bridge
I'll run smiling through my tears

And we nestled three together
In our bed but did not sleep
Crying, whimpering the night passed
Day arrived. Our sorrow deep

You came back in wooden box
With your collar, aqua sweater
Charlotte found a sequined photo
No more heart pain, stormy weather

Little girl you were my joy!
Always watching, always there
Please know just how much I loved you
And I miss you. I'll be there

Gifts and Betrayal

The presents that I gave my Mother
Were oft unused and not unwrapped
Navigating gifts was tricky
My efforts meant I wasn't slapped

Nonetheless gifts unaccepted
Piled deep in closets, drawers
Made me question why I did it
Kept on trying, buying more

Finally did it! Gave up shopping
Just sent money for her choice
Then she didn't cash the checks
And I was left bereft of voice

So I tried to stop the giving
And for sure receiving too
Some folks just kept on insisting
I sent less and less, it's true

Have no interest in the boxes
Bags with bows beneath the tree
I just want the smell of Christmas
Ornaments so dear to me

I did think this time was different
Old dog died. She's full of grief
So I sent massage in check form
Purpose? To provide relief

Thought she could receive my gesture
Of support and kind concern
She's unable to receive
Has to reject, control. Can't learn

Called her out on her behaviors
Denied! Rejected! She is Right!
Is for her a way of being
Control and posture quite uptight

Betrayed again by false persona
Triggers pain from long ago
When my gifts were all rejected
Dad, Grandma, Mimi stole the show

Hours spent on careful shopping
Were dismissed with silent look
Babysitting dollars wasted
Nothing pleased them ever. Took

A lot of therapy and time
To reduce the pain of years
All activated once again
Found the memories and the tears

I release the memories painful
Just an echo from the past
I have grown beyond this woman
Pain released just cannot last

Relationship was unsubstantial
Spirit fantasy not for me
I will change in moving forward
Seeking Truth, Reality

More recovery for me means
Yes to me is No to you
You'll be fine with your denial
I won't miss you. Sad but true

You've your walls to keep you shielded
From Reality you deny
That's okay. You do it your way
I might wave when passing by

Mean and Hateful

Some folks are just mean and hateful
That's how they wake up each day
Complete disregard of others
When confronted . . . they run away

They cannot play nice with others
Nor help anyone new to learn
Work solo. Not good team members
If questioned, others are spurned

You will not find an "I" in team
A concept not everyone knows
Be careful when choosing your team
Avoid seekers of glory and show

Maturity age five to fifteen
Treat others as if they are dirt
Unconscious they muscle through life
Uncaring if others are hurt

Stories they tell are as victim
"Poor Me" they cry to the crowd
Folks have not seen them in action
Gossiping, lying out loud

Stay far away from folks like this
Being nice won't change who they are
Avoid rudeness and stabs in the back
Seek others with love in their stars

Confused Aging

Much of aging does confuse me
Nothing seems to stay in place
One part hurts and then another
Change occurs at rapid pace

Ankle swells for no good reason
Then my wrist and then my knee
Hurts or aches, disturb my sleep
And then I'm fine as I can be

Some Truths I thought were set in stone
Outlined the boundaries of my life
They're now displaced in shifting sands
With normal redefined as strife

Black is black and white is white
With varied shades of gray
Confused the edges shift then merge
Pattern seen just fades away

Swirling clouds of lies like dust motes
Blur my vision, hurt my ears
Truth requires concentration
Track it through the chaos, tears

And I keep aging; time is passing
Minus road signs, missing light
Wondering if there's a reason
I do journey into night

A Friend That Wasn't Really a Friend

I'm sad now. We weren't really friends
It looked like we were from out there
Walled off . . . your secrets stayed hidden
Just superficial was shared

None allowed to really know you
Your busyness always a wall
When sick you withheld information
And contact. You weren't there at all

Weeks would pass. Nothing but silence
I sent cards, emails and I phoned
You didn't care I was worried
Your control absolute on your own

Suddenly learned you had cancer
Then A-Fib that damaged your heart
Used "pickaxe" to gain information
Got email chaotic from start

Too insane/intense for one reading
Overwhelming out of the blue
After three months of silence an answer
Too painful to read and too true

Your caretaking was an addiction
Your choices shortening your life
One way street. No room for friendship
Just ongoing chaos and strife

Realized I never knew you
Our friendship was all in my mind
I'll daily pray for your healing
For my sake I'll leave you behind

My Inner Child

Yesterday my five year old
Came out awhile to play
She giggled eating lemon cake
With raspberries piled high to stay

Like jewels in a crown unworn
Tarnished, dark and out of sight
Now polished, shines in red-gold hair
Her laughing eyes so clear and bright

She stayed awhile and now she's gone
She's deep inside my heart
Her sparkle will not go away
Because we'll never part

I finally found my Inner Child
She knows she's free to play
No censorship or pain again
So she has come to stay

Free From the Fourth Commandment

My father was a brutal sadist
Mother leaned against the door
While he beat with belt and buckle
I would fall from lap to floor

No one there for me to turn to
No safe place to hide away
Mother Silent! No protection
No safe place. I had to stay

Don't ask questions we won't answer
Only ask that stuff at school
I was told, "Dad really loves you."
Never bend or break the rules

Lies they told me didn't make sense
At my questions they would scream
Go to bed and keep the door closed
Don't disturb us with your dreams

Had to kneel at dad's bedside
Every night to say my prayers
Hard to say 'I love you daddy'
When my butt hurt . . . wasn't fair

Still they fought and lied about it
Screaming heard throughout the block
 Only Barbara called them on it
They were silent like a rock

Barbara didn't know he beat me
'Til my sixties—far away
So she couldn't call police then
Waaay too late. He'd had his day

Always hated Fourth Commandment
And the God of whom it spoke
Why would I need two such fathers?
One was too much as I choked

Always sick while I was child
I did miss a lot of school
But my mother—such a phony
Convinced teachers all was cool

Anorexia at fourteen. And
Bulimia followed on
Forced to eat too much I showed them
Now I swallow. Now it's gone

Home was hell as I was aging
Now I'm sixteen. I can drive
His control was overwhelming
Ran away to stay alive

Thought the Army would return me
After college. Terrified
Found a husband. Dad was angry
At my wedding he just lied

Never went again to dad's house
Lived in fear he'd come to mine
Came in eighty. I had blackout
No more contact. That was fine

Feeling better after his death
Cannot hurt me anymore
Accepted that he could not love me
Not my fault so close that door

Mother couldn't love me either
So of parents I had none
My poor body always hurting
Looked for love from even one

Won't forgive them. Will not do this!
Find it hard to go to church
Pray to Jesus. Hope He hears me
Pray that for me He does search

Hoping Truth will lance my abscess
Flush away the pus and pain
Set me free from years of history
Let the Past flow down the drain

Re'my Turning Three

Re'my he turned three today
A special breakfast. Usual walk
The years pass oh so quickly by
Sometimes I think that he can talk

He tilts his head off to the side
And watches me so hard
He's smart and oh so sensitive
Intrigued by his backyard

So many smells. Small paths to take
Or he can run real hard
He listens when the other dogs
Talk, howl, bark in their own yards

Gracie comes to play today
Her Mom will have champagne
A celebration all around
In safe, secure terrain

I'm really glad that he's my dog
We sleep so well at night
At seven he is down to stay
Next morning cuddles tight

Today to Therapy Came God

Today to therapy came God
He knew my need to help her heal
I listened hard and spoke my truth
Her tap root grew; the Truth was real

Vision replaced her blinded sight
Truth collapsed her fortressed walls
Old lies dissolved to dust, now gone
Alone she strides down hallowed halls

Hers! Sanctified through work and tears
She's learned to walk and to believe
To walk with others sharing life
She's learned to give and to receive

Lies From my Mother

I was angry at my mother
Long years after she had died
It was deep corrosive anger
Based on mountains high of lies

She lied to me of childhood—mine
That I did not recall
I've no memories 'til fourteen
Trauma blew away them all

She lied about most everything
There was little truth or fact
She never answered questions
There were no answers in her act

She leaned against a doorway
While my father beat at will
She did not stop him, protect me
Her mouth was never still

From her I learned to lie a lot
Especially to stop pain
It didn't work. Somehow they knew
Beat me twice as hard again

I was their scapegoat—only child
Many secrets in our house
Hours/Days of vicious fighting
I hid in books, a quiet mouse

Only achievements got me praise
Their standards way too high
Normal was not acceptable
Excuses—more like lies

Increased control when I could drive
No trust was ever there
And I could not trust them at all
Spied on me; knew my everywhere

I drove to church to get away
Returned: police were waiting there
Was not believed, "Just went to church."
Don't be selfish. Keep folks aware.

Doubted I had classes so late
Scheduled papers mattered not
Pounced screaming when to home I came
Inside I hated. Deep the rot.

Christmas was a joke that year
They honored NOT my one request
'Twas what they wanted that I got
Unheard again! So poor my rest

Soon after that I ran away
Took clothes and books. I wasn't there
Called: Her almost suicide my fault
Returned. Six weeks—a different where

They kept my car in punishment
I flew to college far away
I married early. They were mad.
Alone on Graduation Day

Stayed angry at the two of them
As they divorced and made new lives
Lived far away as I could go
Dad shed a couple wives

Still thought my mother innocent
And still believed her lies
I floundered in my ignorance
She functioned as a spy

Betrayed me years, and years and years
I learned some Truth 2001
And much more in '09 and '10
Her death 2006. I'm numb.

Then I read Alice Miller
Learned my life had been ALL lies
None forgotten. Some forgiven
Help from The Meadows. No more spies

I still today work on those lies
My patchwork past so full of holes
I write new poems to fill the gaps
Nurture my soul. Tomorrow whole

A Crisis Addict | Compulsive Caretaker

Drama! How some folks do love it
Thrive on chaos! Seek out more
An addiction like all others
Intensity's the hallmark for

These folks. All aspects of their lives
Busyness and multitasking
Crises sought out every day
Seeking those who do the asking

Please fix this! Give control away
These folks so love to come to save
Simple solutions not their style
They prefer to rant and rave

And stir the chaos all around
Exhausting to be there at all!
Predictably health crisis comes
Can't fix the mess when they do fall

They refuse to learn a new way
Even at the risk of death
Don't care who they inconvenience
Creating crisis their last breath

Relationships can't work like this
Ocean storm surge lies in wait
When the waters look much calmer
Crisis sought. Won't hesitate

Outside perspective? They look helpful
Quicksand unclear to average view
Learn the first time. You can't change them
They cannot be there for you

Relationship ephemeral
Best to go. Look from afar
You can clearly see the fireworks
Keep your distance where you are

Outgrowing Relationships | Losing Friends

Outgrowing relationships: Painful
Losing friends not what I had planned
All was the same 'til it wasn't
And I on my own feet now stand

Relationships end without warning
Or maybe I missed all the signs
We were not growing together
Our rhythms no longer rhymed

Conversations had nowhere to go
Directional markers were lost
No longer on the same page
Unseen the eventual cost

Somewhere and somehow I had changed
My eyes saw a whole new world view
Peopled by those yet unmet
Some old friends did not have a clue

Stayed on Merry-Go-Round of the Past
Pushed it to go at top speed
I watched as they rode round and round
Unaware of their wants and their needs

I'm aware and my living is NOW!
Not then. No repeats or re-runs
Will not get on that ride again
Now it is MY time to have fun

Cannot carry you any farther
I have to leave you behind
I'm sorry I could not convince you
To get off the ride; out of line

You've got too much baggage for me
Mine gets less and less every day
I work at releasing my past
And for your well-being I pray

Good-Bye now and thank you so much
For all your support and help too
I couldn't have done it without you
I'm so grateful that you were you

I wish you could see what I see now
And would join me on this High Road
Where I'll walk 'til the end of my days
And carry a feather-light load

2020

The King Wears No Clothes

Thinking's altered. Most compelling
Politics are sharp with thorns
Both sides bleeding. Winning's foremost
No one listens. Rally horns

Loud then louder. Then more strident
Moving cars plow into crowds
We are right and you are wrong
Violence, voices blasting loud

With shifting truths, evasions, lies
Misinformation left and right
Divisive not diversity
Social fabric stretched too tight

It shreds. More gaps. Few bridges seen
Us and them defined and stark
Delusion waves its flag on high
Democracy gets dimmer. Dark?

We few who see the Truth today
King wears no clothes the child shouts!
And glasses rose do shatter fast
Liberty does fade from in to out

America's collapsing now
The glue that held us tight all gone
Death stalks among us high and proud
Strong principles at last ground down

Dictatorship looms ever near
Trump's lies and rallies hype the crowd
Brotherhood a worn out word
Lies and more lies scream out loud

I'm Afraid for My Country

I'm afraid for my country
I'm sad for those who will die
Trump has learned nothing from Science
Whatever he says is a lie

Attendance at rallies spreads covid
When most folks aren't wearing a mask
To stop the spread, to save a life
Is this really too much to ask?

Some world populations wear masks
Their leaders obey all the rules
Except in the US of A
Our leaders are such glaring fools

What will it take for a wake-up?
Four horsemen! Apocalypse ride
Behaviors must change now today
I know not the when of the tide

I'm in Fear

I'm in fear. I watch and wonder
What new mess Trump's making now
What he'll break—perhaps forever
Cannot lose. Does not know how

He's a blob of white hot rage
He's desperate to roll back the clock
To '16 when he was the winner
Losing. Lost. Horrendous shock

He will destroy all that he can
In dangerous childlike rage
Assassin's bullet helpful now
Or a sturdy iron cage

I hope Democracy survives
Another seventy days
Pray God . . . please intervene for us
In all your myriad ways

Trump's a Criminal and a Loser

Trump's a criminal, a loser
Six million people told him NO!
We want you gone from here forever
Go to court. Play golf. Just go.

You're trashing our democracy
Can't go lower than you go
No integrity or honor
Six million people told you NO!

Those within the toxic bubble
Do not care for other's lives
"Covid is a hoax" they say . . . and
Thousands die . . . do not survive

Intent only on their pleasures
Fifty-five million travel, roam
They ignite new covid hotspots
Overwhelm those left at home

They reduce the population
Of the World and USA
Can't replace those we have lost
Lots of sadness in today

Republicans now are losers
They have sold both mind and soul
To cult of disinformation
Six million people said NO!

Lies

How the lies start to fray my own thoughts
As they disintegrate down
Into morass, muddied eddies
Of lost, wasted energy, frowns

Only Fauci stands firm and grounded
His information sustainable, clear
But no one is listening now
MAGA shouts him to silence, boos, fear

Do your part against covid today
It's not safe to go crowded places
Statistics reflect what they say
Need masks to cover our faces

This is NOT a game to be played
Cemetery has become king
Misinformation, lies abound
Who's brave? Who'll stand up in the ring?

And confront all the lies out there
Designed to cause Death and Pain?
Anything's ok to win
Round Robin so ugly again

And 1,000,000 Americans died from covid

Racism—Newly Old in 2020

Feelings buried, stagnant, old are
Now volcanic, molten tide
Erratic pattern—here then there
Live on camera . . . cannot hide

Everybody sees the footage
Men engage in killing act
As though what they did was nothing
All Lives Matter . . . not just Black

Racism's Old! A poisoned plague
A rotten river underground
Clear logic, thought are enemies
To change this pattern . . . sight and sound

Religious roots are watered too
Men kill and die for White is Right!
It's not and never has been true
Yet many boast and bolster fight

That flattens some into the dirt
While others in their mansions thrive
Wasteful "want-nots" have it all
And many struggle to survive

Mindset changes must be active
It's WRONG to be the way we've been!
We can change and teach our children
Clean that river NOW, AGAIN

Engage the law to stop the violence
Stop the hatred sewage source
Leadership and Be Example
Commitment. Change our present course

So much healing—Start today
Stand up tall and say ENOUGH!
Look hard at what you see and read
Clean up words and acts. Be tough

Our World Has Changed

Our world has changed with borders vanished
No! Untrue! The borders CLOSED!
To block a foe invisible
Unseen by any. Sidewalks hosed

What happens when the whole world's changed?
Where are our landmarks, guideposts, lanes?
Forced to search in inner spaces
Unfamiliar pathways, names

Full-time rat races end with shock
Ahead vast Grand Canyon waits
Or tiny trail . . . go left or right
Narrow, hills, rocks, mud . . . no gates

We're alone. It's unfamiliar
No one there to hold our hand
View is iffy. Road uncharted
Seem to be in different land

Somewhere I hear people running
Some are Lemmings . . . OFF they go
Gene pool numbers rearrange
Silence sharp . . . loud cries, shallow

Wealth cannot halt these new harsh laws
For folks who won't police themselves
Entitlement has met it's match
Laws stopping death. Not fairies; elves

I hope there are some lessons learned
As we embrace a brand new earth
Priorities? Please rearrange
So we can all enjoy new birth

Little Truffles Girl (A Poem with Tears)

I miss you little Truffles girl
Your happy spirit, play
You didn't stay too long with us
Made pee-pee all the day

You tried so hard to make those pads
And sometimes you were so good
Then lakes or piddles everywhere
You did the best you could

Something inside just was not right
Infections weren't corrected
And you and I did all there was
Before Jennifer and I connected

To send you back for further care
More than I could provide
To treat you with advanced vet help
To make you well beside

I thank you for the joy you brought
You were special and so wanted
A hard-to-care for puppy girl
But I—I was undaunted

Until the day the vet did say
That inside you were broken
My heart broke too. I made a call
You went away—Tears unspoken

I miss your bouncy run and play
And bark and whine and all
I know I won't see you again
Or answer to your call

I'll cry again and think of you
I tried so hard to win
For both of us and Re'my too
We lost. It seems a sin

So now I won't see you grow up
With your little tiger face
I need for sure to let you know
There's none to take your place

It's way too quiet in this house
And Re'my doesn't play
I miss you little Truffles girl
I miss you lots today

Betrayal 2020

Betrayal when it's unexpected
Deeply wounds. Complete surprise
No defenses. Thought unneeded
Bleeding you look in their eyes

Stranger's gaze intense unyielding
Words spill forth with cold control
Who is this who cannot hear me?
My soul boat rammed on rocky shoal

It's damaged, cracks can't be repaired
Integrity has vanished
Detritus is all around
What was abruptly banished

And so I'll mark the gravesite well
And visit it no more
And older, wiser venture forth
Towards new untraveled shore

Approach with caution. Boundaries strong
Go slow, observe and learn
So I don't hole my boat again
Or crash and bleed and burn

Hope
Requested by Donna

From whence comes Hope in darkest hour
The one in midst of night?
Untethered it is always near
Too often out of sight

And yet in recess of the heart
A tiny flame does glow
Unquenchable, it stays the course
And we can trust and know

That flame of Hope will still be there
When all else does seem lost
When evil seeps from every pore
And we do count the cost

Of giving up or giving in
Instead we stumble on
We follow flame lit in our hearts
Hold hands. We're here not gone!

We rise again with heads held high
We triumphed o'er the dark
Days bitter, long and nights were cold
We guarded close that spark

Of Hope that flickers, never dies
And calls us out each morn
Show-up and do your part today
New life, more Hope reborn

The way it was is over now
Some cleansing has been done
'Tis not enough . . . the battle's on
Til every war is won

With Kindness not with genocide
With ears, and hands and hearts
And step by step we'll changes make
So there are more new starts

That can replace old bloodied stops
Where rancor ruled with pain
Now understanding has a chance
To not U-Turn again

So guard your flame and tend it well
Keep clean your spark of Hope
So you can to the future walk
On gentle, uphill slope

Where all of us can walk abreast
All equal, helping hands
Together now so sun will shine
On all our various lands

Yes! HOPE for all to live and be
Unfettered all our days
That tiny flame is ever there
Will be with us always

Your History and the High Road

Your history has made your Today
Reactive? Reflective? Your call
Hot pain where none was intended
Past face/voice cloak speaker in thrall

You're GONE back to Then in a flash
Fuzzy! Fire! You think it is Now
Lashing out feels great at the time
Comes remorse, then guilt at the how

Did I take that false trail again?
The flashing Stop-Sign was lit
But I plunged beyond . . . I WAS RIGHT!
Ran hard straight ahead . . . didn't sit

And wait and reflect on my goal
Be Present! Not trapped in the Past
Did this to myself . . . another
In mud with the pigs I stand fast

To fall off the High Road so easy
Climb, repair breech, hard to do
No traffic jams on the High Road!
I walk it for me and for you

Thoughts

We run out of time in our lives
Think we can cram more in our days
We push, pack, and pull 'til the bag's overfull
Seams split and all's jumbled sideways

Chains

The morning's here. It's come again
There's the usual things to do
To feed the dogs and let them out
Meds, glaucoma drops not new

Season changing, body aging
I can't do what I did
Perplexing things before were clear
Where are the glasses that I hid

So I could find them . . . just right there
And my list of things to do
I know it's handy, close somewhere
Is it maybe nearby you?

Evaluate my old routines
Have tos, s*houlds*, wrapped in *musts* mast
What helps me stay within the Now?
What keeps me chained to Future, Past?

Crises and Friends

Crises and courage are teammates
Each to the other well yoked
We need them to get through this life
Friends help with the pieces that broke

Emails, phone calls, flowers, cards
Plus shoulders to cry on and hugs
Friends help us get through the crises
Steadfast when Life pulls out the rug

And then we crouch low in the void
Friends offer both light and a hand
They're there as we work to stand tall
And we're sure that they understand

You're blessed if you have friends like this
Not those who use Duty and rod
To prove you're defective, not right
While you're sobbing your heart out to God

So cherish the Truth of your friends
Give thanks and ask blessings for all
Remember you're also a friend
Who runs to support when you're called

Acceptance
with gratitude to Lorie for her wisdom and her counsel

Acceptance minimizes anger
Replaces previous chaos
Defines whose choice is now in charge
Releases hard, trapped feelings, loss

Acceptance is Life's center mass
Place where all beginnings start
Know Great Truth. "It is what it is"
Originates from God in heart

Acceptance not an easy path
Takes strong will to walk that line
Allowing others choice to choose
Their own lives they will define

Consequences come with choices
Some surprises, some are harsh
Some are wonderful, fulfilling
Some result in quicksand, marsh

All are lessons learned with living
Hope our choices mostly wise
Nonetheless, the goal's Acceptance
Of choice within another's eyes

2019

When Trauma Reigned

*I dedicate this poem
to the therapist at the Spa on Oceania's Marina
with gratitude.*

When trauma reigned my eyes grew dim
My hearing, taste, smell too
Touch was foreign. Speech regressed
I wasn't me. And who are you?

Who cares? Will read old books again
I let my mind slow down . . . go slack
Got through another day that way
And I don't feel what I do lack

Food dwindled down to bits and bites
Water intake also low
Took too much energy to live
Alone, I lived so slow

For sake of dogs I had to walk
And feed. Throw toys and balls
Sat in my chair for hours on end
No interest—none at all

Always so tired with lots of naps
Hard on puppy young and small
He made me move to bring him joy
His cheerful smile became my all

My memory was growing dim
I was forgetful too
I couldn't generate concern
Nor ask for help. From who?

And on this voyage at the Spa
Was therapist sublime
Auravedic was his art
He stopped the drain of time

For I had lost the will to live
No challenge, purpose, goal
This place so unfamiliar
I almost lost my soul

Body-mind was not connected
Energies were stuck and stopped
Everything was out of balance
Massage releases came with pops

Pain as things were reconnected
Spirit present once again
Every day now has new meaning
I'm alert to make new friends

I am grateful for his kindness
Expertise, compassion too
Old parts into new creation
Life has meaning. Life is True

Quiet

Quiet in the midst of Autumn
Birds are singing. Traffic roars
Dogs are wand'ring in the garden
Leaves are falling, more and more

Here and there bright blossoms twinkle
Purple, pinks, red-hot pink too
A frog hopped into my kitchen
Helped him home still damp with dew

Blower breaks the morning stillness
Someone's yard now clear of straw
I wonder what today will bring
Crows in neighbor's yard do caw

Not sure yet I'm feeling better
Path seems clearer just ahead
I will go forward—cautious, pausing
Leaves are falling, falling, dead

Pursuit of Honor

When in doubt I watch and wonder
What to do or not to do
When to speak and when to listen
Being? Doing? Which choice true?

Seasons come and seasons go
Time is fleeting, ever swift
Weather changing. Body aging
Path obscured as sun/shade shifts

I am growing. I am knowing
My Today is all that's here
Am I present in these moments?
Do I isolate in fear?

Wake up now! Be Here and Seeing!
Hearing, speaking, smelling life
Running, walking, playing, laughing
Time is Now. Play drums and fife

I'm So Sorry
(in answer to a poem from Colleen to her friends Rolf and Mary)

I'm so sorry . . . I'm so sorry
That this is happening to you
Didn't ask for. Don't deserve it
This Reality is true

Cannot mend it . . . Cannot change it
This hand of cards put into play
Can just grieve the major losses
You're enduring day by day

When I think of you I'm crying
There's so little I can do
Lots of questions without answers
I wish none of this was true

I have memories of years gone by
When we traveled, where we went
It's so hard to leave you standing
In the shadows . . . thoughts unsent

When I watched you as a young man
With your family in your prime
Now my heart hurts when I see you
Helpless there with fractured spine

I will help however I can
Help to help you have a voice
But I cannot run your life now
Can't revise or change your choice

Feel so helpless without power
To control or change the game
I'm just me here with my doggies
No direction—all are same

I'm so sorry I can't do more
If I could, it would be done
You have all my love and caring
Prayers, compassion under sun

When the Time Comes

My Time is Here and it is Now
I am finished with what was
No more waiting. No more asking
No more answers like "Because"

I won't go there. I won't do that
I'm in charge now in this game
I don't yet know all the answers
I just need to Know My Name

It is mine now, not another's
No more hiding in plain sight
Time to Be! I'm done becoming
Purpose found now. Get it right

Speak my Truth and hear the answers
From the Universal Source
Waiting, wandering time is over
Use MY wisdom. Plot my course

It is Now, NOW! Not tomorrow
Dump these burdens. I am free
Blocks have crumbled. Path is open
Meet the world as really Me

I have paid my dues to others
Now unclipped, my wings can fly
Fresh the sunrise o'er horizon
Time to live free 'fore I die

2018

Grieving to Peace
*Dedicated to friends and classmates
and instructor of Grief Week,
The Meadows, July 30-August 6 2012*

I'm sad and sorry! Grieving
How I've lived my life! My voice
Was rarely heard by others
And I lived in Fear not Choice

I'm in Pain! I see the pattern
God, it's awful seen intact
Other's pieces jammed together
Fantasies and not the Facts

I thought, "It's me who's not enough!"
It's Me who needs to twist and turn
Efforting to change for others
Please them when my insides burn

In silent rage I stuff my feelings
They do not see the light of day
I do use my own addictions
They run my life. I do not say

My Truth or share my feelings. NO!
I'm not certain what they are
Don't know names or categories
Feel like wishing on a star

It's just easier to do that
Than to say just how I feel
That's too hard and way too painful
I might have to see what's real

And that hurts to much to go there!
I'll just hide or run away
Lots of choices how to do that
Try again some other day?

Are you listening? I am talking
Telling you just who I am
Can you show me that you heard me?
Nod your head. No silent slam.

I am crying trying to reach you!
It's too late. You're gone from me
Shattered dreams we had together
Future looks so dark. I see

Gleaming glimmer of tomorrow
When this wave of pain hits shore
Then I'll breathe again and smile
Changing how I do keep score

Gratitude will be my focus
What I HAVE . . . not what I lost
I will cherish every day now
Counting joys instead of cost

That's enough to tip the balance
Moderation is my goal
Laughing, thriving as a lifestyle
Nurture body, mind and soul

Path to get her hurts like Hades!
No one walks it due to choice
Take the first step! Choose with Purpose
Speak your Truth in your own voice

This is how our grief is conquered
Truth and Strength move us to Peace
Pain, addictions are not needed
Crises end and traumas cease

Thanks to classmates and The Meadows
Opportunity in Time
We have learned and grown together
Jennie processed it in rhyme

So goodbye to strangers, friends here
Thank you for your "hearts with ears"
You have blessed us on our journeys
Thanks for hugs in midst of tears

We've become friends who are thriving
Worked with Courage all this week
As we celebrate together
Comrades found what they did seek

So goodbye with many blessings
Follow path and choose your star
You are wished the best forever
Peace and Joy where 'ere you are

Time to Say Goodbye to My Beloved Boy

It's now, today, I'll say goodbye
The time has come to let you go
Forgive your dying. I'm alone
On to a place that I don't know

These seven months have been like hell
Wake-ups something hard to do
The day ahead is empty, blank
So much because I'm missing you

I've done much that I don't recall
Cobwebs clog my memories
Not being present for my friends
Has saddened them, my anger, freeze

Awareness slipped into my mind
I saw it. Had to face the fact
I was cocooned in anger's web
And I was stuck. I could not act

I had to forgive you for dying
My grievance had to be released
So I could go forward with living
Somehow and somewhere to find peace

I'll take down your photos and cards
Find a place special to hold
Close by your collar and ashes
Memories of you sixteen years old

I cry as I write this goodbye
Forgiving's like dying again
No more kisses or hugs from you
'Til I see you . . . a long time until then

I thought I could do this today
My heart it is breaking in two
I will have to wait for awhile
Until I say good-bye to you

My beloved boy how I miss you
I don't want this final good-bye
That's already here in this room
I'm blocking and telling me lies

If the cards are not there you are gone
Your picture is in every room
How can I put things away?
The light will fade out in the gloom

Of my life . . . and my heart will crack
Into pieces too small for the glue
Just fragments of dust will remain
Not much there for me or for you

I know that this I need to do
To begin a new journey that waits
For me to take steps to tomorrow
Before I am come to those gates

Of Pearl . . . they stand tall on the hillside
Awaiting all comers with Joy
Someday I will come there to find you
My Camus . . . My Beloved Boy

Six Months Old Today

Today is Re'my's birthday and
He's full of spunk and spice
The doctor said to rest a week
He doesn't think she's nice

Jumps up and down off furniture
No matter what I say
Chased his own tail around and round
Then flopped. Yipped "ouch" today

If in his crate to rest awhile
He howls and gnaws the door
I walk him slow around the block
And he demands Encore!

He's full of baby energy
Nighttime? He is quiet
He barks for breakfast—seven sharp
Ten pounds running riot

Beneath the Snow . . . Beyond the Storm

"Beneath the snow . . . beyond the storm[1]"
Lie unknowns we wish to know
Path oft is rocky up and down
With fear and faith we forward go

We cannot know what lies ahead
Past images lose substance, form
We stumble, learn along the way
Through shining sun and blinding storm

Our path is long. At end is death
Change challenges day after day
Our respite's brief. We move along
We sit in silence. Kneel and pray

What happens when the sidewalk ends?
That is a story writ by you
In colors bright or dull and grey
What future dream could become true?

"Beneath the snow . . . beyond the storm"
These two are part of every life
We face them daily. Friends do help
They bring to us both peace and strife

---

[1] From: *Healing After Loss* by Martha W. Hickman

Camus
By a Friend

Camus was Jennie's favorite boy
She can still see his favorite toy
When his death came knocking at the door
She prayed to God that he would soar

The last few months
He had trouble with his walks
But he'd listen with full attention
When they had their talks

He brought her such joy to her life
It will take a while to bury the knife
I know her heart is breaking
As her very soul is aching

She said it feels like life is in slow motion
But Camus is sending a loving potion
The sun will shine once again
As Jennie begins to make amends

Why did Camus have to leave so soon?
His love for everyone filled the room
Clients would come to cuddle with this therapy dog
As his presence helped to lift their fog

There will never be another
But with time, she will find Jolie a brother

My Grief is Less Today

Today my grief is less than was
My pain and tears less bitter
Today I'm not so overwhelmed
Sun on raindrops glistens, glitters

Today my guts don't clutch in fear
All knotted up and tight
Today my brain is back on line
Status change: from flee, freeze, flight

Today I see some colors bright
Smell oranges in the air
Old photos seen with gratitude
I notice what I wear

My hearing's better. Eyesight clear
Frontal cortex now in charge
I'm back in my resilience zone
Released Dissociation's barge

Overwhelming pain, despair/Grief
Catapult us into FEAR
We cannot heal ourselves alone
Community of friends who hear

Can help us find our way again!
Grief therapy so dear
Rewinds our story . . . heart and mind
Ahead our path is clear

And Step-by-Step Time moves us on
With memories in hand
Of all the joys that we did share
Camus at Rainbow Bridge does stand

Why Now?

Why now, today does pain appear?
That funeral over long ago
In misty past it sits and waits
For me to finally say hello

Bear witness to what was back then
Finally face reality
With understanding, knowledge see
Connections really true for me

Others may not see them plain
A different past the path they walk
They, too, connections have to make
Or suffer repetitions, talk

It's Now the time to action take
To open wide that padlocked door
To where I've hidden all my fears
Face one by one. Say Nevermore!

Will you clog cells with traumas old
So I'm restricted, cramped in pain
I'll stop Denial! Face the Truths!
Hard work 'til I am Me again

Or was I ever Me before?
In thralldom to my history?
I squeezed through corridors so small
Mind/Body not combined you see

That's past me now. I forward go
And times of Fear, Anxiety
Won't hold me back as they did then
Ahead I glimpse my Future. FREE!

Gratitude
for Mike Winslow

I heard my father died today
An old-time neighbor called to tell
When he was seven, I fifteen
As babysitter—I was swell!

He searched computer mysteries
To find me. Let me know the end.
His mission one of gratitude
'Tho sixty years, he's still my friend

The laughing hours of long ago
Memories bright, easy to find
Knew Dad and I were long estranged
Sought to bring me peace of mind

My dad died just the way he lived
One up and always had to win
I took Free Will and gave him his
To live his life and not be kin

Oh Gratitude. Thy gift is great!
Unexpected light of Grace
Thanks so much Mike. You are so kind
To brighten, light my space

I Sat in the Garden

I sat in the garden today
Sunlight gently fractured by leaves
Silence and peace gentle 'round me
I'm healed. No longer bereaved

Camus, now in Spirit, is here
With his unconditional love
How I miss his face with those eyes
He waits for me somewhere above

He may have been chosen as greeter
As my father crossed Rainbow Bridge
For his love and exuberant Joy
Guide for others to top of the ridge

The church bells ring in the distance
Melodious music to hear
Muffled traffic sounds in the air
Life pulses not far away—near

Circles of life keep expanding
Choice to join the flow or withdraw
Welcome each morning a new day
Full of gratitude, humble, in awe.

Collapse of Grief

*Dedicated to friends and family
who supported me in various ways after the death of Camus.
Thank you each and every one.*

Last night I did collapse in grief
My tears were painful, streaming
They're always there. Just on the edge
In nanoseconds, gleaming

I've lived like this near eighty days
Time does and does not heal
I face life one day at a time
Thoughts, memories so real

I'm sure it was just yesterday
I hooked his harness up to walk
That harness lies o'er ashes now
Camus no longer talks

To me, his message clear . . . Hey Mom
Get up and feed me. Breakfast's due
And it is time to go outside
I've kissed your face. Get up. Please do.

And down the stairs on in my arms
Roll over, sit and smile
Race to the door. All set to go
Outside to sniff awhile

His medicines, then half an hour
Colostrum. Finally food
And then he'd beg to walk outside
Hurry please. Walks are soooo good!

And then he could not walk so far
And I would bring the stroller
And he would walk or ride like king
I denied him getting older

And then he walked just round the block
Still looked and acted young
I denied my heavy care of him
Surprised—one day he did run

Through open door I saw him seize
Foam at the mouth, drool, fall
He couldn't walk. I carried him
To vet with urgent call

He'd had a stroke, got meds, IV
I left him for three hours of care
I picked him up and brought him home
My mind a blank some hours there

I wrapped him up in blankets
And I put a diaper on
He licked my nose and went to sleep
I held him close the whole night long

He died so slowly in my arms
By morning end was near
Joyce drove me with him to the vet
Released from pain and fear

I held him close for three more hours
I cuddled, kissed and talked
The crematory van did come
Took him for his final walk

And then came box of ashes
Table full of cards, plant, roses
White for Camus and red for me
Photo. Empty harness closes.

Charlotte sent angel for his box
Cards, calls came from all directions
Books on Dog Heaven and Healing Grief
I couldn't face reflections

Colleen reached out—pushed her away
And many others too
Lorie shared a trauma resource
Hypoarousal—info new

Debbie took and framed a photo
It is always near to see
I'm grateful for friends reaching out
To guide me back to me

I think I'm grieving Ruggles too
Scenario the same
I did avoidance too well then
Buried grief and pain and shame

I now think that I want to live
Jolie licks away my tears
Moments brief of peace do come
Support does fade my fears

To each of you who helped me then
I'd like to thank you now
I'm moving forward day by day
God's light my path, my how

I Choose

Some movies are not meant for me
With too much violence, pain
Radiating off the screen and
Suddenly I'm trapped again

In those scenes I've put behind me
Struggled with Recovery
Lots of tears and then Forgiveness
Trauma triggers Not to see

That world is not of my choosing
Mr. Rogers more my style
In Kindness, Love, Compassion, Peace
I'll immerse myself awhile

It is my choice. My inner me
Seeks soothing solace, Grace
I sit or walk and soak it in
Absorbing deep in body, face

My glow ... benevolence and smile
Reflects now out to others
It lights my way. Brings calm and peace
Freely offered, never smothers

I Love and Loved You My Brother

Death arrives. None see him coming
Heedless of our wishes, plans
Quietly he takes our loved one
To a far and distant land

Death has no place at our table
Yet he takes chair as his own
He's arrogant, presumptuous
We're shocked! In Pain! Alone!

I'm glad we made new memories
The old ones battered, worn
Were put aside like yesterday.
And now I'm free to mourn

I'll miss you in my life of Now
So wanted you to share
My memories I'll cherish, hold
And one day I'll be there

To join you where the rainbows go
With friendly clouds who lose their way
We'll know each other instantly
By what we do and what we say

One of these days I'll say goodbye
Not today. No, not today.
I love and loved you my brother
This now my mantra as I pray

The Cost of Change

Change may not come with happiness
Instead it's drenched in pain
So much hard work to make the change
Now no reversal! Change again

Some folks respond with backlash hard
Demand return to status quo
The price is high to stand your ground
When telling Truths and saying No

Life happens and then people change
For sure they cannot stay the same
The High Road splits—each to her path
And friendships lose their former names

These life demands are very sad
Full of loss and pain and grief
At what point did I lose my way?
Or was it Change and new Beliefs?

I'm right where I'm supposed to be
Another change awaits ahead
No denial or avoidance
This will continue 'til I'm dead

STOP

Light extinguished. Someone died
Their soul no longer here
An empty space. No shadow now
Shock! Silence. Burning tears

The world should stop its turning now
Just now my world did end
The world out there seems just the same
But I've lost my dearest friend

My Tiny Warrior

My tiny warrior gave his life
So I would re-evaluate
My driven style with blinders on
Always running . . . never late

I've always had a goal to reach
And didn't stop till it was mine
Did not see then what I did miss
Just there ahead was Finish Line

Too busy for the dogs I owned
Missed daily walks and cuddles, play
Tomorrow I would play with them
Tomorrow came too soon. End days

He's gone and I do miss him so
Miss kisses and his soulful eyes
I do not get another chance
I was too busy. Told him lies

I did the same to all of them
Empty promises like rain
I'll walk you when I've finished this
And that and that, again, again

So glad that I was not a Mom
I would have done the same to child
I did it too to husband three
So busy, busy! That is me

I'm in a rut that I prepared
Thought that I could do it all
Now I look back with deep regrets
My broken heart in pieces calls

Camus—come back I now have time
Too late. Too late. Time's gone
Oh my Beloved Boy Camus
I regret what I have done

I read too many, many books
And didn't hold you near
Just sometimes looked into your eyes
And thanked God that you were here

I promise I'll do better now
For love of you my boy
I know I can't turn back the clock
You were not a wind-up toy

You couldn't wait for me to learn
You couldn't wait and stay
I'm slow to see Reality
And slow to learn new ways

I'm sad I was so seldom there
To hold you and to play
And when I cross the Rainbow Bridge
We'll do that all the day

I hope you can forgive me now
With Re'my I do play
And hold him near while I do read
And walk him twice a day

We spend a lot of cuddle time
Together—nighttime too
My lesson learned Beloved Boy
Wish you were with us too

Your picture hangs beside my chair
And sits on old armoire
I kiss your face beside my bed
And love you from afar

You were my tiny warrior who
Tethered to my soul at night
So it could not get lost in space
With you on guard, eyes so bright

I still miss you tiny warrior
I hope you run and play
With other dogs who used to be
Together in my heart you'll stay

2017

Today's the Day My Best Friend Died

I hate today. My Best Friend died
A sudden stroke with damage
His priceless personality
Is gone. How will I manage?

He's wide awake; he maintained watch
All through the night in bed
With lots of kisses and good-nights
Then off to sleep he led

He loved his harness and his walks
And rides in stroller too
Walks became too hard for him
I don't know what to do

I hate today! My empty bed
Tonight will be like hell
I cannot sleep. I toss and turn
And cry. My heart's a shell

I'll love again, but not like this
Two hearts were really one
And mine is raw and bleeding hard
I feel empty. Done

How Tall You Stand
for Susan

When and where and why don't matter!
Life just happens. Things go wrong.
Midst of mess pick up the pieces
Step out with right foot, left . . . move on

Is there blame? Of course, there's plenty
Can't be erased nor clock turned back
Your approach needs to solve this problem
Is the key here? . . . gray not black

Find your North Star, your solution
Consult with others in the know
Can't be hurried . . . your solution
Time Takes Time! And goes so slow

That's okay! In here's a lesson
Challenge: You're to change your ways!
Your old patterns will NOT work now
Process! Plan! Then have your say

To your new language, style of speaking
Others will now listen, hear
You have taken charge, control now
Mastered! Set aside your fear

Resolution will go forward
Outcome may not match past plan
Doesn't matter. Problem is solved!
Oh, how you've grown! How tall you stand!

And I Wonder Where You Are Now?

And I wonder where you are now?
Jumping, dancing in the rain?
Free of aging, can you play now?
No arthritis, tumor, pain

Without you I am so lonely
In denial you're not there
Can't accept you won't be waiting
When I return home from somewhere

Your basket lies lifeless and bleak
Silent, empty there on the floor
No need to lift you up or down now
No way to help anymore

You left me so quickly . . . no time
So few hours, they just sped by
Here then gone. No preparation
Crying and watching you die

I thought our future was always
Lied to both—to you and to me
I still am not in acceptance
Not how I thought it would be

Ashgebat Turkmenistan

The sun arises o'er the trees
Between the buildings marble white
It's on its own. Free with the birds
All else is regulated, tight

The lights go off on monuments
Splashing fountains sparkle and gleam
The cleaners sweep and mop by hand
A silenced army, faces seamed

Quiet boulevards and streets
No bleating horns or traffic jams
Parks unpeopled. Benches vacant
No music, voices. Police cams

Are everywhere on building tops
Recording, spying all below
And crimes are charged! Reality!
Cannot escape. No place to go

Airport's illuminated bird
Few passengers. One hundred staff
Passport check at least six times
Stern, quiet faces do not laugh

The City Of The Living Dead
Façade o'er crumbling buildings old
They're empty—an impressive show
Egoist statues painted gold

Legends worshipped, history altered
The goal—a nation to create
With rigid rules and camera eyes
The price is high for Police State

The Golden Princess steals it all
Basis: tons of natural gas
Poor planning empties Aral Sea
Arrogance claims both future, past

The Turkmen horses gleaming gold
Their prancing feet on drifting sands
The centuries will come and go
And meld anew these desperate lands

Both poverty and children's plight
Are lost midst palaces and greed
Future arrives and payment's due
For all the lives they did not feed

Today

Today I think I'll write a poem
Unsure of what subject will be
Words tumbling out, coming forth
Don't seem organized logically

So into the melee I wade, I
With my pen and paper in hand
Directional signs I don't see
In this strange and foreign new land

I know I was not here before
Did my old place get rearranged?
Is it me? I'm not who I was
I'm different! I've radically changed

So from new perspective I see
A world full of colors and light
Misty, gray veil has vanished
My choices are so often right

Oh! Wow! I'm walking the High Road!
Recovery now I can claim
Left behind shadows and darkness
Now I own and honor my name

I'm PRECIOUS! I Love Me! It's true!
I finally rejected old lies
My path's free of potholes and rocks
Today sunshine bright and blue skies!

What Comes in Silence?

What comes in Silence, cat's paw soft?
A whisker's touch or simple thought
Am I alert or sound asleep?
Then finally the "what" is caught

And resonates as I receive
This new awareness, point of view
Judgment vanishes like smoke
Compassion blossoms in me—new

Silence serves as transportation
For message, music from the spheres
Those far beyond my human ken
These come to me year after year

I'm TOO busy for the Silence
Patience? Waiting? Not for me
I am driven . . . tasks to do now
Highlight! Text that message—see

Oh, I missed it in the volume
Of the data on my phone
Wonder if it was important?
When I text I'm not alone

Anyway, this Silence scares me
This NOT Doing . . . quiet place
What will I miss while I am here?
In the mirror . . . just MY face

Silence in the world around us
Needs a space within us too
Nurturing who I'm becoming
Silence lets me see you're You

I'll see you as individual
Let you be you and not my clone
I'll celebrate our differences
And common ground will reap as sown

The In-Between

The time of In-Between has come
I'm deep within its space
Both walls and floors are fluid here
I sit and pray for Grace

My "Doings" finally are contained
And I can sit and Be
This change is really hard, hard work
To finally stop and Be

I have been running all my life
A busy, busy bee
I surely got a whole lot done
In doing lost my Me

Sadly I thought I was checked in
Instead I was checked out
I didn't SEE nor FEEL my life
Some days I hid—did pout

I always rushed to places, things
Crammed more into my day
Refused to stop! Declined to slow!
I had to have my way

And then I ran into a wall
Was over Everest high
And wide and deep. It stopped me cold
I had to change or die

Dr. said it was colitis
Autoimmune mixed with stress
Was my life over? Travel done?
Poor sleep. I was depressed

This was a major wake-up call
Caused by the way I'd lived
Oh—it took years to get to here
Addicted so to give

To get a dose of Self-Esteem
From others—outside in
To be the hero—save the day
And I did lose—not win

See Self-Esteem comes from inside
I generate it all
If I don't make it for myself
Comes illness, then I fall

I'll age and die before my time
If I do not say NO
And take charge of the life I have
And set my dial to slow

I will still help. Stop rescuing
My boundaries need work
They're my authentic life support
Without them I'm a jerk

And heedless of my wrecking ways
To others and to me
Boundaries guarantee my health
Protect my sanity

And so I turn off Run and Do
In silence and alone
I quietly seek other ways
And to myself atone

For being somewhere else—not Here
Within my span of years
I vow to be participant
And sometimes there are tears

For all I've missed along the way
Can't walk this path again
I vow I'm here for me this time
I'll be my own best friend

I don't much like this In-Between
I know I need to stay
My path will then reveal itself
And I'll be on my way

I am Precious—It is So

What's it like when someone tells me
That my therapy is done?
Codependence to Recovery
War is over! Battles won!

Oh, I'll walk with healthy fear now
Vigilant . . . not hyper state
Take in data from my worldview
Process. Reason. Things can wait

'Til I've thought through my best choice now
In confidence, serenity
No more rushing, multi-tasking
Take my time. Decide for me

My Day-Timer will look different
Lots more spots for me to play
Gratitude list in the morning
And at end of every day

Watch my language! Wall of Pleasant
I can be just who I am
I can live within the moment
Stop my whining! Be a clam

If I can't say something kind
And Respectful to you when I speak
Then it's best to keep my mouth shut
Less the mess when I don't squeak

Point my finger, blame, resent you
When the world does not me heed
Check and see myself in the mirror
Learn what I do want and need

Pia's way is so much better
Than the ones I've tried before
Time is now to restart my life
So I'm walking out the door

Thank you Pia for the process
For your years of work and toil
Your ideas germinated
Found within me fertile soil

Help and guidance were provided
Classes, CDs, training, books
And I slowly learned your model
Time and study, those I took

To find self within the wreckage
Of a Past so long ago
Found the jewels deep within me
I AM PRECIOUS! It is so

On the Other Side of Forgiveness

Forgiveness comes and in its wake
Comes Freedom too and hand-in-hand
They bond with Boundaries we've learned
And in this space we understand

Denial's gone! What was is True
Grief's torrent comes. Acceptance here
We pray for help in Letting Go
The shackles fall. Release the Fear

And pain and shame and anger too
With deep breaths and sighs depart
And gently flows fresh sun-kissed stream
Forgiveness from the heart

There's quiet now and peace within
The anger's simply gone for sure
Acceptance now takes its place
Allows me to move on

Old mem'ries dimmed within this work
The painful list of sorrows, wrongs
I can't recall the litany
It vanished. Now it's gone

And so with prayer I contemplate
New gentle peaceful place
Within myself there's innocence
Faith in the human race

And this flows out from me to them
With every word and breath
My motives, energy are cleansed
Remain so 'til my death

My transformation is complete
Can feel and see its face
So much and better place to be
I thank God for His Grace

Trees

My trees dressed up in thanks today
In scarlet, green and gold
And brilliant orange with hints of red
The wind is biting, cold

It whips the trees from side to side
Through branches thin and tall
It rips the leaves where 'ere they are
Ends crisp, they scatter, fall

Dark trunks with barren branches stand
Defiant, waiting, tall
'Tis time for me to sleep away
The days 'til Spring does call

Death

Death I did not you invite
Into my fountained' yard
I locked the gate to bar your way
You bypassed it . . . Pushed hard

A gentle soul as ever was
Will rest within this glade
You came. Took him away from me
His urn awaits the spade

He loved me deeply . . . whole heart through
For nearly sixteen years
I'm doubtful that my heart will mend
So painful are my tears

A loved and loving little dog
His name it was Camus
I can't believe he's really gone
This surely can't be true

I held him as she gave the shot
To send him home to God
I pray he watches Rainbow Bridge
Which one day I will trod

And then we two will meet again
And never more apart
Those trusting eyes. That wagging tail
So much within my heart

For now the tears. I miss him so
He was my life's Best Friend
My path looks dim and difficult
'Til I see Camus again

Bereaved

A cloudy day. The skies are gray
Cold rain and falling leaves
Both sound and light have been switched off
Within folks called bereaved

They shuffle forward. Stop. And wait
And turn to look behind
For shadow . . . echo of their past
A Presence in their mind

There's nothing there but memory
So profound the sense of loss
The time they had was not enough
Dirt clods with ashes tossed

Silence . . . Another wave of pain
Tsunami blocks the sky
The ground does shift . . . then rearrange
Is it too soon to die?

The road ahead looks bleak and dim
My purpose absent, gone
Where find I signposts, comfort, light
And strength to carry on?

I'm told that healing comes with time
How long? How long my wait?
The sunshine's missing in my world
I'll leave ajar my gate

Poetry

Poetry is language for the
Feelings I can't name
They're hidden deep in tissue, cells
Lost in the past with blame

Awareness and good therapy
Will sometimes help them choose
To leave. Yet those deep buried ones
Can rupture . . . or they ooze

And I am caught so unaware
Of massive change inside
With fingernails I hang on
When end comes after ride

And then I'm in some peaceful glade
Serene and quiet now
I'll rest awhile and then move on
My poem will show me how

From Tied-In-Knots to Letting-Go
Grand Canyon chasm wide
Without a path or bridge to cross
I much prefer to hide

This Change so Strong. And I was weak
In thinking of my past
Now I'm across and walking on
The High Road . . . here at last

2016

Trauma Reaction

Nanosecond strikes with violence
Memory replaces Now
Five years old within that instant
Clueless . . . knowing not the how

Name for this Trauma Reaction
Shame Attack can walk beside
Helpless child. Alone, bereft here
Adult vanished . . . like the tide

All those memories come thrusting
Out of blocked and hidden doors
Colors, sounds and even smells come
Also words heard 'oft before

Emotions come too: Shame, Fear, Pain
Sometimes they overwhelm you
And take you hostage . . . blink of eye
So hard to then explain to

Another who reached out to touch
To comfort or remind you
And now "wears" another's face here
Behind and not beside you

There's no intent to follow-through
With some words of hurt or shame
Or actions that are base, unkind
While calling you bad names

Stop excuses. Don't resist.
Your body keeps the score and memory tells true
So stay in Here and Now . . . Not Then
In Recovery for you

Blame and Relationships

Blaming you isn't the answer
Nor back generation or two
Yes! I can see how it happened
Passed on to me . . . same as you

BUT! . . . Somewhere here there's a new choice
When rose colored glasses are off
Now no Denial, distortions
This data's researched so don't scoff

I will be making a change here
I will get angry . . . Say NO
Don't look so shocked! Past is over
New rules enforced. Start the show

Equal in volume, opinion
NO! No more shouting me down
When I ask a question . . . please answer
Do your share of planning and sound

Respectful to me with your speech
And when you are listening too
Then we will have conversations
Instead of your face turning blue

Discharge your rage somewhere else please
NOT in my lap or my space!
This you do own! Take it back please
I see the look on your face

This is responsible sharing
This is relationship's core
When we are equal and loving
Few folks could ever want more

If not there are consequences
My health does matter to me
I won't live in rage and confusion
I'm seeking Serenity

I'll work on my issues and problems
And trust that you'll do the same
Then we'll go forward together
While we are sharing one name

I hope you will see that I mean this
Serious as a heart attack
Listen to me . . . take some action
I simply cannot go back

Back to the way things were done then
The times before now lived with lies
Please take my hand and walk with me
First I'll look deep in your eyes

I'll pay attention to actions
They "Speak" much louder than words
I'll see the imbalance believe me
Listen! For I WILL be heard!

Circling The Wagons

I circle wagons in my brain
Resist reality
So I can deny what I know
And what I will not 'See'

This works awhile and then doesn't
I crash into a wall
Open eyes . . . embrace Denial
Now . . . so familiar a fall

This NOT the outcome that I planned!
My expectations so high!
How came I here to Sidewalk's Hole
With Me, Myself and I?

Out damn DENIAL! Out I Say!
Return you Not Again!
Cease I the circling of my train
Reality's my friend

Strays

Are you a collector of strays?
Focus on others to save?
You're needed wherever you go
Endlessly like ocean wave?

Where is the cry you are hearing?
Is it near or far away?
Cry from a child or an adult?
Drop what you're doing and say

I'm coming! I'm coming! Hold on!
Life saver here in my hand!
No fighting . . . I'll tow you to shore
Soon you will be on dry land

And still you want to be carried?
Okay . . . there's just a few stairs
Up the steps too? You are whining
Knees give out. I have gray hairs

What am I doing with my life?
I'm tired! No energy
Gave it away to the others
Didn't keep enough for me

Worn out! Used up! I am old now
Health is beginning to fade
This is the price of my choices?
For Nursing Home. . . .Coffin . . . I've paid

Wait! Is there time? Do it over? No?
No returns are allowed!
Only this one life is given
Yes! You can start Today . . . Now

Wake up! Pay attention to you!
Don't rescue! Hold out your hand
Those who want help . . . they will take it
Go forward together . . . And

Let Go of the others behind you
Trust that they have different road
Let them walk on at their own pace
Not your rocks! Lighten your load

Teachers, Competence and Humility

What happens when I'm competent?
What do others say and do?
Some of them are threatened and they
Squash me right under their shoe!

It does not seem nice to say this
Still it is so very true . . .
When you can do just what they do
Then they are so through with you!

It never made much sense to me
I thought that was the goal
For me to become competent
Mature and even whole

They didn't like my competence
Preferred I stay in school
And never really graduate
Or they could look . . . a fool?

I think they're all mixed up inside
Need to sit on a throne
With others genuflecting fast
Creating little clones

Becoming individualized
Is not part of their plan
It smacks of independence. And
You forget to hold their hand

See, individual competence
Means you've grown up at last!
Then take the reins of management
Within Your hands . . . hold fast!

Become in charge of this your life
From others walk away
If they are threatened by your skills
Keep going! Do not stay!

'Tis they who need to learn . . . Let Go
Say my job is over, done
I've taught them all I have to teach
Bless and wish them days of sun

And hope they have umbrellas by
When stormy weather hails
Makes piles and potholes on their paths
And no wind fills their sails

The teacher comes when student is
Prepared and ready . . . asks
And then it's time to leave again
Leave student to Life's Tasks

For teachers competence do teach
Then get out of the way
Let them succeed . . . fall down . . . get up
You've done your job today

If you are threatened by their skills
You have a lot to learn
I'm glad my lesson is not yours
When Humility you earn

Clarity

Clarity it keeps on coming
I'm not seeking. It's just there
Where it comes from I don't know
Present. Bright. And I'm aware

That the way I used to see things
Isn't how I see them now
So much changing in the moment
Sometimes hard to process. Wow

It's not more than I can manage
Need be conscious . . . fully here
Cannot dawdle in confusion
For the future's very near

With new path for me to walk on
And this path it's marked with lights
No more stumbling in the darkness
And confusing blacks and whites

It is waiting . . . right ahead there
New my future . . . bright sunbeams
Rainbows stretch out in the heavens
On them walk . . . hold on to dreams

Clarity . . . it has its moments
Friendships clash 'gainst history's door
Is it opening or closing?
It is time to ask for more?

Is there more here for the asking?
Has for this one season passed?
What is in it for us both now?
First a prayer . . . then peace at last

Consequences of Texting

Life moves faster. More fragmented
All do hurry, scurry, rush
Shift their focus . . . check their I-Phones
Cannot for a minute shush

What's the hurry? Where IS the fire?
Do you know how stressed you are?
Hear the ping and send the text
Now! Even when you drive the car!

Can you die while texting/driving
YES! It happens every day.
Your kids do it 'cuz they copy
What you do not what you say

Where's the crisis you are chasing?
Is this one you did create?
Take a moment to reflect here . . .
Then don't overload your plate

Are you living in the fast lane?
And exhausted more than not?
You're the one to put the brakes on!
Stop your spinning on the spot

At your family time in restaurants
Do you all sit there and chat?
Or is each person on their phone
And just texting where they're at?

This is surely Not connection!
This fragments your family ties
That you are Not creating with
Your loved ones. And by and by

You will want a conversation
To know deeply who they are
What you've taught them they have learned well
You'll want near and they'll run far

Compare texting . . . conversation
One's together, one's alone
Think you well before you choose here
And perhaps pick up the phone

This busyness it is your life!
Life's not a dress rehearsal
So Take Time For Your Life Today
Or health will do reversal

New Ways

I rarely think negative thoughts
That isn't how it used to be
I wallowed in pity . . . my own
Whined over and over . . . Poor Me!

Refused to stand on my own feet
I wanted to lean hard on you
Or maybe be carried awhile
On high here there is quite a view

Each of us gets just one childhood
I wanted another right now!
Fact: I did not want to grow up!
The Truth was I did not know how

Many the reasons from childhood
Role models were limited, few
They were just kids in big bodies
And they did not know what to do

So they passed on Codependence
I was a great student, adept
Things did not work well in my life
I was grumpy. I overslept

Issues at work plagued my days now
Reminded me so of my folks
I am repeating their stories!
Sarcasm's not funny in jokes

Since I don't know many grown-ups
Just how do I learn what to do?
I'm done with this Merry-Go-Round
I'd like to grow-up. Be like you

I gather I need some new skills
My tool box is empty and light
First I learn Boundaries . . . Then what?
I need to learn that I'm not right

When I give advice to others
That I don't practice for me
I'm hypocrite and dishonest
And I want to trustworthy be

I'll keep my mouth shut and listen
Observing the wise in my world
Journal, read, meditate daily
And grow up to woman from girl

Need to learn how to do money
Responsible for how I live
Need to watch my health and diet
Learn how to receive and to give

So much to do every day now
There's so much that I need to learn
Responsible for my Self now
My Self-Respect I need earn

Task for responsible person
Yes that's Me! Becoming her now
I'm learning as fast as I can
Thanks so much for showing me how

I found a grave for Denial
And buried Illusion there too
Though tough . . . I finally did it
If not I could not learn from you

This will be my task forever
For sure till the end of my days
Thank you for walking beside me
You taught me to live in new ways

Controlling Me

Others do try to control me
And I bite hard, scratch and fuss
Inside my "Oh So Nice" façade
Truth is . . . I am a wuss

Why is it that I don't speak up
Truths that so are mine?
I do fear confrontation . . .
And stay back . . . behind the "lines"

This is a pattern I resent
First taught when I was small
So hard to break . . . I do it still
E'en now when I am tall

I really want to tell my Truth
Could you simply listen?
Please do not tell me what to do
Yes! . . . these tears do glisten

You do not see it as I do Okay!
Your eyes, they are not mine
It is Okay to different see
And think. Don't start to whine

I'm learning to speak up for me
I'm not stepping on you
When you see white and I see black
Right's not the same as True

What's True for me or True for you
They may not be the same
If it's a big production then
We need not share one name

Folks grow apart or they grow close
When different paths they take
As years go by we different are
With health and lives at stake

So please control yourself! Not me!
It is a mighty task
The same that I set for myself
And this I do but ask

Treat Self with kindness . . . same for me
And I will do the same
The world will be a better place
With Truth. 'Tis not a game

Children

*Dedicated to Children Incorporated In Richmond, Virginia
where I have sponsored children for 51 years.*

Children! Our hope for tomorrow
Children are our legacy
What kind of world will we leave them
Bright future? Sad history?

Unheard are voices of children
Crying with hunger at night
Unemployed families have hardships
How can we help? Make it right?

Children they need education
Learn how to read and to play
When Poverty is their playmate
They may have nothing to say

When we can give help to children
Then their eyes light up with hope
Caring compassion supports them
Gives strength and courage to cope

With all the issues in their lives
With which they have to contend
Parents disabled or missing
Sponsorship means there's a friend

Someone from somewhere is sending
Money for breakfast! For shoes?
Supplies for school? A new jacket?
They're special. They did not lose

The chance for a life that is different
Diploma opens a door
They can have books for home reading
Maybe learn a music score

Children they wait on the sidelines
Will someone show up today?
Could you please help me? I'm lost here
Take my hand . . . show me the way

Old Soldiers Sing

I think on the places I've been
What I saw, felt and heard and where
My world grew and opened my eyes
Expanded my consciousness there

Lands ancient with history old
Religions and temples so vast
On plains, mountain tops and in caves
Flags fly free atop the tall masts

There's water and cleansing and prayer
Candles burn, flames flicker in jars
Incense wafts to heaven in clouds
Chimes, bells, songs, call to prayer heard afar

Though different . . . some places have peace
'Twixt neighbors who are not the same
In others less tolerant . . . NO!
Forced change . . . even war . . . in God's name

Old soldiers hang on to their past
When young they did fight for their dreams
Now proudly sing their country's song
Salute others who sing . . . smiles beam

I've grown, stretched and gathered new thoughts
Seen dances and stories so old
Still living through children today
Rich tapestries adding new fold

Bali and Java
Thanks much for inviting me in
Hold on to your values, your past
To change too much would be a sin

Shadows Of Shame

Shaming shadows fall upon me
Heavy weights do hold me fast
Leaking out of ancient doorways
From a childhood's distant past

In that moment . . . isn't distant
It's immediate . . . and Here
Today's the voice . . . within this instant
Now I'm overwhelmed with fear

Shame! I curl up. Die inside.
And Crawl or Freeze? I cannot run
Perhaps I Fight! Strike out with rage?
Or Flight . . . like bullet from a gun?

This Shame's pervasive. Takes me down
Taught by parents long ago
I couldn't ever get it right
Those double-binds of yes and no

I tried so hard to perfect be
Fear both Failure and Success
Brought worry to a state of art!
Deep inside . . . I am a mess

That niggling imperfection that
I try so hard to conceal
It trips me. I fall down again
Try for Perfect more than Real

And I . . . I just can't live this way
Can't sleep and my health gets lost
Within the game I'm trying to win
No failures or I'll be tossed

Out of this family! All alone!
Abandoned! Can't survive!
Imperfect? . . . I'm not loveable!
What's the point to be alive?

This message . . . it is just NOT true
Perfect we can Never be!
We only need to do our best
Believe this! Now you're free

Tough to embrace our humanness
Perfectly-Imperfect . . . Real
I throw the shame away for good
And now that I can feel

I celebrate my efforts to
Be Moderate each day
And Balance and Serenity
Will help me find my way

Save shame for my embarrassment
Not tsunami passed along
From others irresponsible
It was their daily song

No! Stop! Don't play that song again!
It no longer bears my name
I'll celebrate humility
No more cowering in shame

Belonging To Myself
Dedicated to Marianna ... thanks for your idea

I am not someone's property
I Do belong to Me!
I am not someone else's clone
And I don't always see

The world the same as they do see
I see different . . . not the same
A generation separate from
Those who gave to me their name

'Tis not for me to live their life
Do what they did not do
I've choices to make for myself
And to myself be true

'Tis not for me to live their life
Do exactly what they do
I cannot wear the shoes they wore
Or see the world they knew

When they were age I am today
It was a different year
The Clock of Life can't be rewound
Do not make new old fear!

I need grow up to be myself
Perhaps will not have child
Okay new pattern to create
I am contained . . . not wild

If I was someone's property
Then I would not have rights
To Be and Do as unique Self
Pay bills for gas and lights

Sometimes I struggle to define
This me defined as I
Takes lots of work to grow me up
'Tis project till I die

I love my family and my name
Please remember . . . I'm Not you!
I will remind you if I must
In your heart you know it's true

Consequences Of Choices
—The Price We Pay

Nothing within this life is free!
And things do come with cost
Delusion!...when we this deny
And overwhelmed and lost

We seek solutions from without
When they are found within
Or seek we others...life to blame
When we lose instead of win

Takes time to see the price, the cost
Attached to every choice
Most often it is hidden well
We're 'oft bereft of voice

The choice looks good from outside in
All's well and tidy...tight
And then we're deep in Twilight Zone
Confusing darkness...night

The carrot bright upon the stick
Does beckon us to taste
How much is fantasy? Mirage?
Slow down. Be not in haste

If it looks too good to be true
Stop cold! Now look again
Your price may be too high to pay
Your soul may be in pain

Can you afford to pay this price
If you must pay your soul?
When you do reach your journey's end
Was this an honest goal?

Or are you holding ashes sour
From fires you did walk through?
What's left of your integrity
And where's the you that's You?

Illusion is so masterful
And we can be so blind
Beware what can look too perfect
Sign with care on bottom line

Or you'll be sleeping with a frog!
Prince Charming was not real
Yes . . . limerence will do you in
And I know how you feel

With clear mind . . . open eyes and ears
Do Not be you deceived
There's lots of good within this world
So you can be relieved

That you are conscious and awake
You know there's price to pay
When you will see things as they are
Regrets won't mar your day

This is one of the Rules of Life
They are Immutable and true
You may not like it! Still it's real
For all of us. You too!

The Journey

People are so very different
From the moment each draws breath
Struggle to be individual?
Or compliant? Till their death

Each of us does have a journey
Solitary path some days
Destination's not as vital
As the lessons on our ways

No one else is as unique as
Each of us in human form
Even twins . . . well each is different
Subtle tuning . . . separate norm

Still, we journey on together
Members of the human race
Some are faster; some are slower
Each goes at his / her own pace

Lessons come and lessons go as
We do learn along the way
Some sit down and stay right there!
While others race towards future day

I don't know what waits for you on
Path that's yours . . . continues there
You are master of your day and
You are seeker when and where

Bind your fears so tight with courage
That they'll hold when you do fall
Part of life is to recover
Tough . . . if you do have it all

Spend some time in contemplation
And your inner landscape learn
You'll get more out of your journey
With the wisdom you do earn

LIFE! Yes . . . it is there for living!
Start today and celebrate
With gratitude for all you've got!
No regrets! Past time! Too late!

Who is That?

Who is that within the mirror?
To whom does this face belong?
When did I get all those wrinkles?
Sagging chin? Not right! 'Tis wrong!

Age has crept in . . . oh so subtle
Overnight my features change
No! That's false! It happens daily
Youth to age we're rearranged

This part sags and that part's noisy
Crepitus in both my knees
Near and far I need my glasses
Sometimes issues when I sneeze

Then the things I hear sound fuzzy
Now I need a hearing aid
The Dentist gives to me a mouth guard
Youthful tanning? Skin stamped PAID!

Takes me longer to recover
From my efforts in the yard
Twice the trips to empty my car
From my shopping. This is hard!

I get tired . . . Need more sleep now
I'm in bed by nine or ten
Can't carouse till midnight hours and
Ibuprofen is my friend

Get the house cleaned by a team
And note the windows need a wash
Where's that number in my phone book?
Wonder if it's check or cash?

Still I'm walking on my own feet
I can drive and gas my car
I can organize my taxes
If I'm lost . . . not bad, so far

It's okay for me to slow down
I don't need to win this race
Can be present in each moment
Earn the lines upon my face

I'll collect my friends around me
We'll all do the best we can
Support, encourage, carry-on . . .
To each other give a hand

Cement Tracks

Life's stopped me cold. Cement my tracks
When sailing on the seas
Intestinal bug was in control
And I was on my knees

For hours twelve from both ends flew
All my meals of two days
And I was green inside and out
I could not mend my ways

So to the Dr. I did go
A mask upon my face
Two kinds of pills now in my hands
Returned to take my place

Within my cabin sixty hours
As if I was in jail
Santa Marta, Columbia
Unseen when we did sail

My ginger ale was my best friend
For eight and forty hours
Then rice and yogurt, chicken, tea
Could safely be devoured

I slept a lot. It wiped me out
Most certainly alone
I read five books within those days
Without computer, phone

And I am humbled by the power
Of things too small to see
That cut us grown folks down to size
And show us how to BE

Alone in Silence where we are
Since we are not in charge
And sit with Self and Miserable
Gaze at the world at large

Take stock of who we are today
What we can and cannot do
With gratitude that we're alive
That we can see this through

Tomorrow comes Aruba
And I'll count another land
Past days will fade in memory
New basket is at hand!

We're not in control of our lives
We're here by Grace of God
This time I only had some flu
Not this time saw Death's nod

Healthy Aging

Life brings to us current challenge
Tell the Truth! Walk in the light
Say NO with more and more power!
Don't hide in darkness like night

Imperative to remain conscious
Seeing things just as they are
I will not walk in the old fog
My nights are clear with bright stars

Repression steals both health and life
Always to say YES . . . a bore
Your Body-Mind knows this is false
Corrosive rage feasts in your core

Then it erupts in some illness
You are in pain and die soon
When are you meeting your own needs?
When is it you call the tune?

Far as I know we have one life
Don't let anybody live yours!
Take charge and live life your own way
Days vanish quickly like hours

Stand up for Self . . . Use your Boundaries!
Protect/Contain who you are
They save you from illness, dis-ease
Without them sink . . . Not go far

Find those who can hear you say NO
Courteously respond in kind
With these folks it's safe to be real
And you'll keep . . . not lose your mind

Dementia's not part of aging
Represents cost of dis-ease
Stand up for yourself and your health
STOP! Always others to please

Live every day . . . every moment!
Make mem'ries . . . better than gold
These . . . the treasures of a lifetime
Remember . . . smiling . . . grow old

Ending Old and Broken Friendships

Codependence costs me friendships
When I grow and they do not
Stuck in old, 'oft whining patterns
If I stay then I will rot

It is sad and hard to explain
To someone who WILL not hear
That they're going backwards healthwise
Surely seems to me so clear

Such reluctance with Denial
Face and say out loud what's true
Stead of putting blinders back on
Choice that they will surely rue

People come and people go.
And lives do intertwine and split
Sometimes good and sometimes sad
Pages turn and stories writ

What we had in common's gone now
Seems it vanished overnight
That's not true! Eroded slowly
Drop by drop with acid's bite

What did bind us close together
Mesh of interesting weave
Weft and warp disintegrated
Only choice left is to leave

Sometimes words are said in anger
Sometimes icy silence reigns
Sometimes looks convey the sadness
What was lost can't come again

Then a time of waiting . . . Lonely
Existential void appears
This is NOT for faint of heart here
This for those who face their fears

Hang in there through isolation
Look in mirror . . . Who is there?
With new thoughts or patterns forming
Going forward when and where?

Long the time of In-Between here
There are neither markers, signs
Suddenly the time is ended
No more sighs and sniffling whines

Then there's room for folks to come in
You've made space . . . your world within
Come in at a higher level
New the music . . . Dance and spin

Gone are the before complainers
Gone are victims! Addicts too!
Resonance attraction changed now
They are them and you are You

Say good-bye with gentle language
They don't truly understand
That they're stuck in old concrete of
History passed hand to hand

Generation to another
Familiar pattern you did break
This is why the friendship ended
They stayed there and you did take

First one step and then another
Out of history's pages old
It took lots of work . . . was hard too
You refused the lies they told

To maintain their fond illusions
Even ones they grew to hate
You removed those dark sunglasses
They kept theirs. Now it's too late!

For the friendship that you once shared
It can't handle truth and light
Courage is Fear that says its prayers
And you know for yourself you're right!

So you honor them in memory
Wave at them across the street
Let them walk with equal others
You have some new friends to meet

Where they'll come from? I don't know
Truth: Universe is in charge
Take deep breath! Have Faith! Keep walking!
Future comes: enhanced, enlarged

Solutions and Problems
With gratitude to Reverend Tommy Sweeley, Methodist Minister,
for his sermons in July of 2016 which he graciously shared with me

Solutions are different than problems
Though they are connected at heart
Removing glue that is so stuck
Does take us right back to the start

Some see problem . . . old solution
Doesn't work . . . they do it more
Spinning so fast they can't see it
Reality's shoved out the door

Doesn't mesh well with Denial
These concepts are way far apart
Denial 'seems' more powerful
With matters of the heart

Give others many excuses
When what they do hurts us inside
We 'Stuff it" or nagging we whine
Our Boundaries flung far and wide

"Oh, Houston, we have a problem"
My solution . . . it does not work
The walls of my life are crumbling
And sometimes I act like a jerk

Need new Solution
My mind is fresh out of a plan
My feet in concrete . . . I struggle
Will anyone give me a hand?

Need to rethink my Solution
I think it is the problem here
Certainly it is not working
And I am surrounded by Fear

I take my own inventory
My consequences are not fun
Need face this! Admit to myself
The Problem is ME! I'm the one

The only one who can change this
Bring chaotic life to controlled
Stop my dysfunctional choices
And get back in touch with my Soul

Find therapist who'll give feedback
Bring Spiritual back to my world
Slow down and learn how to listen
Become new Solution! Unfurled

Like new flower I will emerge
New patterns replace patterns old
Chaos begins to diminish
On this plan for my future I'm sold!

Limitless the Clouds, the Sky

When the pain of change is over
Spasms echo lost refrain
New horizons now familiar
Sunny skies . . . and clouds with rain

'Tis not that the change has ended
Change continues all life long
If not changing . . . you are dying
Change your music! Sing Your song!

Fear of change will maintain prison
Strangles you as time goes by
If you don't stretch and reach for more
Few will mourn you when you die

Others need to see you growing
They need models! How it's done!
Fake it . . . take another step and
Cross the winning line . . . You've won!

Yes it took a lot of courage
Support and guidance on your way
And this time you showed up for you
Take your bow and have your say

Tell your story. One will hear it.
All that's needed is the TRUTH
With open eyes and honest tongue
Step and pass through Life's Toll Booth

Leave behind the smoke and mirrors
Of Denial and Old Lies
Some refuse to walk through with you
Embrace sadness . . . Wave good-bye

They now walk another path that
Once to you was common ground
Your turn climbed up to The High Road
Others passed, continued down

To wide roads walked by common herd
In total union . . . no dissent
Exactly where they need to be
No crowds on High Road where you went

Change continues. Turn and face it
Walk upright with head held high
Set your stride towards your horizons
Limitless the clouds, the sky

Time
Dedicated to Lance

What is time? What do we with it?
Since we cannot do without
Do we hoard it like a miser?
Celebrate? Or sing? And shout?

Spend it joyously in living
Every moment of our day?
Waste in worrying? In anger?
And in planning what to say?

Which way gets you to your goalposts
On the field of Your life?
Solve a problem with compassion?
Light a torch of crisis, strife?

Mind you well your use of time!
And the same for others too
With respect be honest steward
And expect the same for you!

There's no bank for extra hours
Minutes, seconds fleeting pass
Use your time ever so wisely
Pause and look at you in glass

Celebrate the seasons seen there
In the wrinkles of your skin
Hoping that you're all the wiser
And no longer have to win

All the games that folks do play now
With the people in their lives
And the hurtful things they do to
Former lovers, husbands, wives

Ever part of the solution
Choice is always up to you
Time is ever, always Precious
To yourself be constant, true

Look on Time as precious gift!
Yours! No one knows how much we've got
Spend it wisely . . . Joy and Laughter
Pretty soon . . . time you'll have not

Being

Being is different than Doing
Being is quiet repose
Being involves contemplation
Peacefully watching day's close

Being means sitting with silence
Nothing distracting around
Being means sitting with feelings
Embracing . . . not shutting down

Being is hard to get used to
Discipline by different name
Stopping your Doing's a challenge
Oh what a difference! Not same!

Practice is called meditation
Usually sit on the floor
Sitting in chair is okay too
Turn off the drama. Now soar

Deeply on wings into Being
Yes . . . you're alone with just you
You're in a sacred Earth space here
Doubts clarified become true

Being reveals your Shadow
Self you prefer to deny
None of us do want to be here
Being's where we can rely

On Self . . . emerging from darkness
Confusion, Busyness too
Being makes time for this process
Being makes you into You

Contemplate internal landscape
Colors and Music are there
This is where Spirit and Soul live
In Peace . . . and Serenity share

When you make Being a practice
Do it the rest of your days
Please share your wisdom with others
Help light their path through the maze

You'll get the help that you need now
When this commitment you make
To Being . . . how you live Your life
It is a risk you can take

Departure

*Dedicated to K and her angel
and wishing her well. It was an honor.*

Clients heal and then they leave me
That is my job! I'm duty bound
Lead them out of their own darkness
To Future that is sane and sound

Teach them skills and independence
To problems solve, make choices wise
Mostly how to trust safe people
And stop believing other's lies

When they do choose their time to go
And last appointment they do make
I'll think one more lesson's needed . . .
I will be quiet. Lots at stake

Best is they now trust themselves
I emphasized 'til they believed
That they were Precious and were loved
And never, ever did deceive

So now I trust that they do know
The path their drummer calls to take
Their Inner Wisdom has grown strong
With feelings real . . . no longer fake

And so I pray for them at night
And daytime too and sometimes more
I taught them all I knew to teach:
To walk the "High Road"—Less is more

To tell their Truth with honesty
Use Boundaries both day and night
To focus eyes on their North star;
Use kindness 'stead of being right

To say their NO as strong as YES
And do Self-Care before it all
Forgive themselves and others too
Help . . . ask for help when they do fall

And so it's time to say Good-Bye
"Joy-Pain" for me and for them too
Please love yourself . . . you Precious You
And to yourself stay ever true

Truth With Honor

When I tell my Truth with honor
'Tis not to tout another's flaws
My Truth shares my reality
It honors my internal laws

I tell you true just who I am
How what you do does impact me
And I may ask you please to change
A preference! Not demand you see

And No! You do not have to change!
Perhaps there is more work for me
Deep work to do upon myself
Clean pain up from my history

'Specially if you did not offend
Mix-up . . . confusion all is mine!
So I'll trot off to do more work
And then all this will be just fine

So then . . . when I've done lots of work
And what you do still impacts me
In negative or hurtful ways
Well then it will be clear you see

That we're not in relationship!
And maybe you don't really care
About me in the ways I need
So we don't have that much to share

And then I'll walk away from you
With gratitude for lessons learned
Though I'll need time to understand
The up's and down's of what I've earned

The same goes forth from you to me
How what I do impacts on you!
Your preference is for me to change
Can I? And still to Self stay true?

And then we start over, again
With the work we both need to do
And growing, learning all the time
Can stay to selves and others true

Each of us is responsible
For cleaning up our history
So it does not muck up our lives
And the relationships that we

Want and need to remain human
Part of mankind's community
Takes some work and dedication
Evolve ourselves and better be

Always tell Your Truth with honor
Please! . . . Please don't climb upon a throne
Or you'll sit there in the silence
And wonder why you are alone

Imagining the Future
With thanks to Pia Mellody
for her concept of "The High Road"

I'm imagining the future
In the process . . . Being born
Past a sleep that I've been leaving
Comes a bright and shining morn

It's been waiting with the shadows
Which direction would I go?
Towards the rainbows or the storm clouds
Honestly . . . I did not know

Mist from past was thick and sticky
Hard to see . . . then wash my feet
Wearing blinders makes it hard to
Really 'See' folks you do meet

And the Seasons, they are passing
Spring is here and Summer comes
I'm now looking. Is he seeking?
Our encounter . . . roll of drums?

'Twill be different this new future
Because I'm a different me
Not impulsive or intense now
From Codependence I am free

No Not Cured! I'm in remission
It is part of who I am
Walk securely on the "High Road"
Every day do best I can

Yes! My future it is coming
Greet with smile and laughing eyes
This reward for all my hard work
Enjoy life! Expect surprise

This is what I missed in childhood
Surprise crowded out by fear
I'm grown up now. This is my life
I'll take charge! My way is clear

I'm okay now. You go your way
Here our paths they do divide
Thanks for being coach and mentor
Thanks for walking by my side

Future's here . . . beyond horizon
Sun is rising clear and bright
I am free from my life's story
My day's here! No more the night

Absent Pets
Dedicated to Suzanne and Lorraine

When I think of you I'm teary
Despite months or years gone by
Seems like yesterday you were here
Sometimes inside/outside cry

You were such a part of my life
So important every day
We exchanged our special greetings
And good-nights along the way

But you ran away and left me!
Long before I was prepared
For your absence. Just where are you?
What a gap in life we shared

Oh I miss you! And my heart hurts!
Miss your precious eyes and face
There's a pain that keeps on aching
Other one can't take your place

You were special! Want to thank you
For the joy you gave to me
Graven in my heart and mem'ry
That is where you'll always be

Someday I will move past this pain
Open up my heart again
Not today and not this moment
Kleenex please. Here comes the rain

Clear Sight
Dedicated to those who are in the process of change

Things have changed past recognition
I don't see what I saw before
With quiet eyes and peaceful face
Now comes the sound of closing door

Intense and urgent I engaged
With pressured speech and strident tone
And racing ran through all my days
I couldn't tolerate . . . Alone

Hooked hard on my adrenalin
I couldn't hear what others said
Some interventions slowed me down
Or I'd be running still . . . or dead

I do not want to say My No!
Afraid of those that I would please
I age-regress and little child
Inside I'm begging . . . on my knees

I cannot see this scene so clear
As caring others from outside
When someone safe does take my hand
I can step forward and not hide

They challenge me to see things clear
To stop my spin and poor Self-Care
They help me grow my Self-Esteem
Encourage me! . . . Strong! Willing! There!

Self-Discipline is up to me
To make the changes they inspire
I DO deserve the Trust they tell
Discard old coals and light new fire

One day I'll see that I have changed
Fear will no longer haunt my night
I'll look my future in the eye
With wonder, joy . . . and now Clear Sight

Grace

'Tis Grace that takes us out each day
And Grace that brings us home
I trust in this above all else
And, therefore, I can roam

Around the world on land and sea
With Faith greet every day
Gratitude list before I sleep
Then bow my head and pray

Exhausted

I'm exhausted from my healing
Long ten years of efforts passed
I'm depleted deep within me
Couldn't know and didn't ask

Knew my brain would do the healing
And my body . . . it would pay
All the insights to my history
Leaning to live in Today

Not anticipation/mem'ry
Those were patterns from before
Hard to unlearn those old lessons
My fatigue reflects that score

I was tired when I started
Didn't give myself a rest
Was clueless that I needed one
Wanted so to be the best

"The Best" at this Recovery
No idea what that meant
I hoped I would find happiness
After all the effort spent

I am Driven! My genetics!
It is who I've always been
It is why I finish projects
Why I lose and sometimes win

I keep going fueled with nothing!
But Determination's fire
And I conquer that last hurdle
Crash exhausted cross the wire

It's a curse and it's a blessing
For to live life in this way
Neither Moderate nor Balanced
So unreasonable to say

That any other should do likewise!
Live insanity as Life
Label this as happy pattern
For a husband or a wife?

No relationship can thrive there
In that erratic, toxic place
They forget they're individuals
With unique and Precious face

So I spend my time alone now
I'm still tired! Not much fun!
What drove pattern I achieved
Always under moving gun?

I suggest you do it different
Not the same path that I walked
Don't be rigid and so perfect
Listen more than you have talked

End of life does come so quickly
Are you ready for that day?
Ready now to meet your maker?
Will you list excuses? Say

Well, I need a little time here
Clean up messes that I made
No? I had a chance already
Well Okay. And mem'ries fade

I'm exhausted! It is evening
Now I need to go to bed
Finally listen to my body
Ear plugs in. "Goodnight," I said

The Power and the I of NO

Who are you? Where are you going?
Do you know where you have been?
Have you learned to say word NO yet?
With your feelings do you win?

What I mean is do you know them?
Every feeling has a name
Do you know its' shape and texture
Or to you are they the same?

If the latter then I am sad
You are missing out on life
All the colors of your feelings
Rich the Joy in midst of strife

No! A word of profound power
NO! Does give to me an I
Separates us with a boundary
When I use it I can cry

Cry in Freedom and Honesty!
No repression to be nice
That repression . . . it will kill me
Lock my heart in block of ice

If you do this for a lifetime
Oh my dear friend you will pay
With disease and pain and suffering
Deep inside you did NOT say

What YOU wanted! What YOU needed!
You pretended all was fine
Thought your turn it would come one day
When it didn't . . . silent whine

Was too late! And Life was over
And your turn never arrived
All the suffering and the serving
Was for whom? Who really thrived?

If you gave away your essence
What was left and did you speak?
Or keep silent . . . rage internal?
Empty effort? Mouse's squeak?

Learn to speak now! Learn to say NO!
For yourself and others too
It is okay to be angry
State your NO and work things through

Get it out now. Don't go numb here
That will kill you day by day
Take your life within your hands now
Be in charge and have your say!

Others may not like the New You
It's OK! They get their turn
To do likewise. It's more honest
Than inside let feelings churn

Into cascade of emotions
And a flood of cortisol
That will trigger immune actions
That will destroy you! You will fall

Into Dis-Ease. Into illness
Stop this pattern. Stop it now!
Live in Truth, Reality
Stop Denial! Please learn how!

Lap Dogs and Thoughts

Camus, Jolie and I sit here
There's one on either side
Hot cup of chai is in my hand
No better place to bide

Awhile in quiet peace with thoughts
About the this and that
Within my tapestry of life
Like dog does chase a cat

Thoughts of holidays and travels
And friends close by at home
And memories of years gone by
When I was not alone

Was life so very different then?
Will memory tell lies?
When focusing on happy times
Will I forget I cried?

And does it matter now, today
What happened way back then
When I was busy, running fast
To myself not a friend?

Yes it does matter!
I believe I'm here to learn what's new
On my path of evolution
While to myself I'm true

Remembering I'm Precious!
And I am a Child of God
And I can be imperfect when
I walk the path He trod

I'll sit here with my memories
And journals. My Today
Can mostly be what I do want
To think . . . do . . . have My say

And when this day is over, gone
And evening's sun does die
I'll know I've lived my day for me!
Deep breath. Contented sigh

True Story
I wish this had not happened to you my friend

When I finally tell my story
Who will listen? Who will hear?
It is painful to retell it
From place of Darkness, place of Fear

Problem is they don't believe me
No place for this in their world view
Thus they deny the whole damn thing
Tell me that it can't be true

They were not there at old Fort Hood
Racism alive and well
White pilots who thought they 'Were God"
Black female nurse—for me 'twas Hell

They threatened me and said they'd kill!
I was afraid and all alone
Reported them to the MPs
Told me to buy a gun . . . my own!

I was a nurse . . . to support life
To buy a gun? This was obscene
I couldn't live within this world
I was alone to cry and scream!

I couldn't sleep. The walls were thin.
They yelled through walls . . . pounded my door
Sat on my bed with gun in hand
I lost my mind. Stared at the floor

I was so stressed I could not think
No place or person safe for me
'Twas hard to work. I could not sleep
Black did not count for much you see

After four months I was a wreck
And my career was on the line
'Twas ALL I had to HAVE A LIFE
I had to go or lose my mind

Transfers AREN'T done at just four months
Takes Act of God to make this so
Avoided situation real
Cut my orders. Let me go

I begged and to Alaska went
No one asked why 'cuz no one cared
No consequences there for them
I buried this . . . with no one shared

And then one day it all came back
And flooded me with memory
I screamed alone and writhed in pain
And Dr. Jackson heard my plea

And he believed me . . . said, "It's true!"
Vicious racism long ago
Was tolerated! Eyes were closed!
Ears didn't hear! Refused to know!

PTSD does run my life
My world's become so very small
Fear rides both shoulders, weighs me down
Help's hard to get when I do fall

Exhausted! This defines my life!
All vets with nightmares know this well
Take meds to sleep. Hard to get up.
And some days life is just pure hell

Is there a place I can be free
From memories entrapped in brain?
A place that I can just be me
Who I was then . . . no trauma stain?

Black Panther

My ring's the head of a panther
Black diamonds with emerald eyes
I bought it so I could remember
The times before made of lies

The times when I couldn't get angry
The times I couldn't say NO
Peter Levine wakes the tiger
My panther's not just for show

Wearing her I can remember
Days when I didn't know Me
Now I can look in the mirror
Tell Truth of whatever I see

No more half-truths . . . little white lies
So you will approve what I say
I don't fear the judgments you make
Or if you choose to walk away

That can happen! Happened before!
Said sorry and ran after you
I will not do that again
My Panther will help me stay true

To my Emotional Competence
Finally established my base
Now that my Tap Root is grounded
Look eye-to eye in your face

Finally meet you as equal
Member of the human race
No more one up or one down here
We share this occupied space

I will assert myself daily
Speak up for ME all the time
My life has a healthy new pattern
My boundaries keep life sublime

Easily express my feelings
No more Repression you see
Or a confused immune system
That attacks 'other' that's me

I'll try to skip MS and Cancer
And avoid Alzheimer's too
Being "Too Nice" sounds a death knell
For health and long life sadly true

Denial obscures the Past
Negative Thinking bad answers
Honesty. Truth. These do last
That's why I bought my black panther

Statement of truth made of gold
Wearing it I will remember
Fantasy keeps me in darkness
Reality lets me grow old

Life and Moving Forward

Life is always moving forward
This day will never come again
Up to us to keep the rhythm
Cannot do U Turns back to Then

People change as time is passing
Do you stand still or walk in place?
Each of us hears different drummer
Are you a runner in Your race?

If YOU run you'll leave behind those
Who stop, walk, sit and dream in place
Learn their wisdom as you're passing
Share with friends in your time and space

Change is often disconcerting!
Where's the stable ground I knew?
In the NOW of where you're moving
Boundaries Bloom. Oh, how you grew!

Process: Differentiation
Out of the herd . . . you're now unique
Often needs some deep alone time
You need to strengthen new techniques

In a time of separation
From the turbid to the pure
Will be times of hesitation
And some days you won't be sure

Almost like a resurrection
The Who you were has got to go
You're becoming! It's a process
Someone, somewhere is in the know

And we're looking for that person
Next Wisdom Teacher on our road
Need the lesson that is waiting
Need help to lighten heavy load

Life is always moving forward
Miracle and where are You?
Can't step in river same place twice
Go forth in Faith! 'Twill see you through

2015

My Story

Now it's time to write my story
What is best for me to say?
How can I explain my journey
Philosophy of Day By Day?

Most of it is way beyond me
Why that focus? Why that choice?
Truly I do not have answers
Poetry did give me voice

Voice? the usual way of talking
Telling others what you think
And feel, believe and understand
Verbal skating on ice rink

With pirouettes and jumps, fast turns
Patterns elegant, sublime
To music heard by only you
Few others hear the rhythm, rhyme

And you connect in conversation
Oh the joy of being heard!!
A taste of heaven here on earth
Conversation's music? . . . Words

So today I write my story
It is what it is for now
More will happen. It's not over
I'm in charge of me. So Wow!

Easter Comes
On Wings Of Song

As the ghosts from Past long vanished
Echo or return once more
Briefly flicker. Gone forever
Healed now and finally o'er

Inner landscape modulated
Steep terrain to rolling hills
All volcanoes have erupted
Spewed towards healing woes and ills

Avalanches . . . all have melted
Trembling ledges have dissolved
Green and flowers carpet hillsides
Emotion's tremors are resolved

DRIVEN! Your absence is noted
Void fills up with calm and peace
Sleep as gentle blanket covers
Nights and days from stress released

New and strange now FEAR is missing!
Yes, of course! Can't less expect
I'll adjust as days move forward
I'll observe for Grace . . . Respect

Gone the days Intense, Impulsive
Off now of that rigid wheel
That locked me into patterns old
And froze out what I think and feel

Now Resilience. I am fluid
Easily adjust my wings
Change my flight path with air currents
No more stuck with stuff and things

Changed the people that I fly with
Few are those who'll fly with me
Left behind those with their brakes on
What's the weather where I'll be

Where I'm present in this moment
Different discipline is this
Takes more energy . . . new pattern
Now! Awake! Aware! first kiss

Birds on feeders . . . others singing
Breeze is cool and sun is pale
Spring arrives as if reluctant
Summer in the wings is hale

So live we as seasons pass us
Aging so relentlessly
No choice that! Can choose how we live
Move in rhythms like the sea

So I wish you Peace this Easter
Can be Easter every day
Comes with parts of resurrection
Grace comes too as we do pray

Feels grand to write a new poem
Sourced from different wellspring now
Sent with love, smiles, hugs and humor
Flights and songs of birds show how

Faith Mountain

When I tell or write my story
Emotions bloom or vanish
Finally, some to dusty death
Long silence now is banished

This road is steep, uphill both ways
View from the top worthwhile
My guides and teachers on my path
Wait there for me and smile

The mountain is well named: 'tis TRUTH
Spelled with a capital 'T'
Those lower hills are built on lies
They no longer work for me

I know I walk against the flow
Fast pace of humanity
I move ahead step after step
Gratitude. Humility

These share I now with folks I meet
In ways both big and small
With smile and hug. I'M REALLY HERE
Can help one by one . . . not all

There only is enough of me
To help folks learn how to fish
I cannot help the world as whole
Despite what I might wish

Help and control . . . way different things
To some they are the same
The folks who do get them confused
Are known by different names

So climb you up your Mount of Truth
Help those along your way
If they are stuck . . . leave them alone
Help someone else today

Another teacher walks this path
Perhaps she's the one who's needed
Recall the Tower of Babel here
Much wisdom is not heeded

The ones you're meant to help will be
So clearly marked with light
You will see them and they'll see you
All's fine and this is right

A Balanced Legacy

Legacy! What is your calling?
Why for do you get out of bed?
Think you always first of others?
What will folks say of you when dead?

What did you do in your lifetime?
Offer help or pass on by?
How will you explain your choices
To your God in Heaven. High

Above us all He watches o'er us
Since He gave to us Free Will
What will we do with gifts given?
He with patience watches. Still

In hope that we will get it now
Today. Not wait until Life's end
That we will live each day with gladness
Helping others, equals, friends

Each of us is born with gifts that
Help ourselves and others too
Balance! There's the magic word we
Need remember. Many, few

It doesn't matter. Each is destined
Walk your path. Hold out your hand
Still and quiet; Speak your Truth
When necessary, take a stand

And back to Balance! There is Grace
It comes in softly, whispered peace
So there's the answer to the questions
Pause and Pray. Then act. Release

Results to God. He's got it covered
Fret and worry have no place
Do your best and Let It Go Now
Stop your spin and end the race

Legacy! Just what will yours be?
Ponder this in days to come
Changes make if they are needed.
Time is fleeting. Race soon run

Less Is More

Less Is More! I need to practice
What that means in sight and sound
How it impacts my decisions
Sleep in? Sight-see? Just sit down?

Book a new trip or stay at home?
What is best for me to do?
Take a walk or sit on the deck?
Read or chat awhile with you?

Choices need consideration
Busyness can trash my life
I can live with light frustration
Calm with Courage. Skip the strife.

Less is more demands attention
Quality instead of lots
Of this and that. I don't need more
Of anything. Oh? Why not?

I have enough. Am enough too
I need to learn to look not buy
Maximize mem'ries in my mind
Richly textured you and I

Was really great to take this trip
Brighten memories from my past
Sausages, Lebkuchen, gluhwein
Now I'm home and need to fast

2014

Choices and Consequences

To each of us there comes a time
The Choice is ours forever
The consequences come along
With fair or stormy weather

Rules of Life

These seem to be the Rules of Life
Rarely fair and wide their range
Flexibility full-time
Stay awake, alert! And Change!

Forgiveness for My Dad

Dad, I understand you better
Than I did in years gone by
Understand the hell you lived through
Wonder why you didn't die

From the hell and long war's trauma
Corregidor, Bataan Death March
How you focused on survival
Through winter's cold, Geneva's farce

On terror, torture based survival
Sick and starved, abused and shamed
How you faced another day and
Kept alive the burning flame

Of Freedom deep within your heart
To see you through another day
Believed God had abandoned you
No longer hoped, felt need to pray

And four years passed while you were gone
And others lived a different life
And you returned and tried to live
You married; had a child, wife

And still the demons festered deep
And few, if any, understood
How you lived compartmentalized
With beating heart but made of wood

You were not there and could not be
Your missing parts left gaping holes
Still you struggled on each day
With disconnected mind and soul

The child I was could not explain
Nor understand your moods of rage
I was as good as I could be
Not good enough at any age

And so I ran away while young
For me Survival was my goal
I ran from you, your rage, your plans
Attempts to gain my mind and soul

To fill the gaps still left in yours
I wouldn't give them up to you
We stayed estranged for thirty years
I cannot trust your word as true

You lied so often, rare the truth
I could not see my way for years
I've learned that trauma traits pass on
Like red-gold hair, blue eyes and tears

I was supposed to live your life
The one you lost in World War II
It simply could not be re-found
Since living well was up to you

Not doing so at my expense
NO! My life was not yours to live
I did the things you couldn't do
But you took all I had to give

Wanted more! Not yours to ask
Or take. I nearly ended mine
You asked too much. I was bereft
And finally, I made My climb

From prison camp that was my home
I grew my wings and learned to fly
My flight was heaven/hell combined
And I learned how to live—not die!

I'm grateful for your lessons taught
My sheer determination! Will!
To finish all that I do start
High is the cost today and still

I go on fuel long expired
I know from whence that gift did come
I thank you for successful path
Of life. Relationships succumbed

I had no skills in these. None taught
Nor witnessed back in childhood times
No conversations, compromise
Just changing rules, lying lines

Of "You do what I say not do!"
That is your job. Mine to dictate
And I will tell and never ask
And only I can be irate

Not you! Your job is to obey
My rules and laws. Do them My way
It's not okay to think your thoughts
I will not hear the words you say

If they conflict at all with mine
Consider them un-thought, unsaid
If you persist on your own path
To me you will be as if dead

And so I walk the Death Railway
And see the videos of war
And understand your trauma source
You need to win and always more

And wish we'd both had different lives
Untainted by the brutal past
And with Compassion I go on
Acceptance first. Forgiveness last

Fog

Change like fog drifts in with tendrils
Insubstantial, wispy, soft
If you've done the hard work, effort
Suddenly a brand new loft

From which view extends forever
New horizons, rainbows bright!
Your hard work has moved you forward
From the shadows to the light

Dissipated! Fog that held you
Fast in grip that kept you blind
Now your vision's clear, unclouded
Enhanced your clarity of mind

You don't like much of what you see
So what is it you can do?
Here acceptance is the answer
They are them and you are you

Change comes daily just like breathing
Coping is a skill that's learned
Some folks do not comprehend this
They're surprised when they get burned

10:00 a.m.

Who I was inside has altered
Sticky webs ripped harsh away
That had trapped me in delusions
"It wasn't what it was" they say

Oh, YES IT WAS! My memory's clear
Reality so painful now
Easier when I denied it
My life energy used as plow

Allowing them to walk away
From Chaos music/dance they wrote
Ignoring impact of their choices
To generation next they quote

"I did it all for you my child"
No time to see you as you were
As special precious perfect child
"You've problems now? I don't concur"

It didn't happen as you say
Your childhood was wonderful
You misremember this and that
I mean it! You were Just a girl!

It takes tremendous courage to
Deny delusion's stranglehold
That deep suppresses Truth and Light
With Honesty the Truth is told

And then the healing can begin
With pus expressed from hidden boils
Dissociation may result
Hold on! Released from trauma's coils

Your frozen self relaxes, thaws
And energetic waves release
They'll carry you to unknown shore:
Serenity and deep felt peace

The Glue of Friendship
Dedicated to Charlotte

Friendships take very special glue
It needs to be renewed
What held together years ago
Flakes off and cracks are viewed

Folks separated grow apart
Live lives walked on different roads
Takes efforts strong to reconnect
Hands paired do lighten loads

Sometimes a crisis brings us close
Sometimes moves us way off-shore
There's grief in changes that we make
Don't really want to close that door

On what was wondrous in the Past
My friend truly saved my life
Her strength sustained me every day
In my world so full of strife

Without her kindness and support
Would have had a full collapse
Because she was so THERE for me
I recovered. Used bootstraps

To get me on my feet. They were
Often applied by my dear friend
And when I walked more steadily
And I was on the mend

She started new life for herself
A gorgeous wedding day
And I was there right by her side
To smile her on her way

And years passed by and miles apart
Slowly glue did crack and split
When I in crises called again
She used her trusty repair kit

Sent cards and notes to keep me sane
Nine years ago divorce
And moving to a place alone
I set a brand new course

She always made some time for me
When I was sore in need
I hope I did the same for her
She is a friend indeed

We're older now. Our lives have changed
Time/distance far apart
Priorities changes as families grow
Yet still we're close in heart

We carry shards of history
Each one for the other
I know my shard is in her heart
And to it she is mother

And loves me for just who I am
When I don't know my me
I am so grateful for her gift
To let me be my ME

For now we'll let the glue that's there
Relax and hold the space
Catch up and chat when life permits
And someday face to face

We'll reminisce of our shared lives
For over forty years
With cookies and a cup of tea
With memories, smiles and tears

And years pass by and miles apart
Slowly glue did crack and split
When I in crisis called again
No time for me, won't use her kit

Broken hearted I said good-bye
I hate to lose my friend
But she's no longer here for me
So sad . . . this is the end

Her husband, family, take her time
And there is none for me
I'm grateful for the years we shared
I wish for her the best you see

Sociopaths

Sociopaths teach us lessons
Adjusted reality
Where is the truth in their language?
What is the impact on me?

Sociopaths lie with each breath
Impediments are not found
Nothing can stop the progression
Deceit lurks in actions and sounds

Sociopaths look so sincere
"Gaslighting" another name
Bewildered, bedraggled and trashed
Victims lose, status not same

Sanity too becomes questioned
No validation at all
Grinning he stands at the altar
Another victim does fall

Sociopaths: one in twenty
Protect yourself! Be alert!
For if you are trusting and blind
You are the one who'll get hurt

Filaments
Bagan Myamar

Filaments within glass spheres give
Magic glow to old Bagan
With stupas and pagodas tall
Nine centuries have come and gone

And still they stand in testament
Of faith in Buddhist ways beliefs
Brick on brick with terraced steps
Statues, art and bas reliefs

Mobile faces, dark hair, eyes
Ancestral image true today
Master artist's careful hands
Used plaster, paint to us relay

Their stories. Truths of ages past
Remain the same. The masses bleed
Absolute power still corrupts
Still fighting wars, still blind with greed

Bagan majestic. Silent peace
Stand tall. Be grounded in your past
Walk slowly into modern times
Be safe at home and free at last

2013

Night Dreams

Now the dreams of night have scattered
Shredded mist with new day's sun
Where to go and what to do now?
Will I begin? Have I begun?

Where's my star? New source? Direction?
What do I know and what to learn?
Begin right now! Begin again
Wisdom needs be worked and earned

None succeed in isolation
Community is sacred space
Take care with your impact on others
Protect the Self to finish race

The purpose is to lessons learn
The colors black and red and white
Reflect the lives we live . . . or not
We choose to live in sun or night

Yes both are needed . . . dusk/dawn too
All moves toward balance strong and true
The compass lives within our hearts
All humans, beasts and me and you

2012

Birthdays

I'm sixty-five and growing older
Don't qualify for middle age
I'm reticent or maybe bolder
Life's passing quickly, turn the page

And suddenly another year
Is present with its aches and pains
That I've ignored successfully
Send quiet signal: Today Rain

It's fascinating to look back
At all the years that lie behind
And speculate on what's ahead
New challenges for body, mind

Required passion is a must
Warm welcome to a lofty goal
Unknown adventures wait ahead
Expanding self, strengthening soul

Accepting change that comes with age
Acceptance comes with Truth today
My choices make me who I am
What I did or didn't say

A Birthday! Greet with gratitude
Today begin a chapter new
Reflect on who you've come to be
Say Thank You. Remember too

That some did not wake up this morn
With gratitude smile through this day
Tell others what they need to hear
What's in your heart . . . don't wait to say

The perfect words. The time is now
Tomorrow comes or maybe not
Enjoy your Birthday Day today
For others have you in their thoughts

Finding Balance

I am stumbling, righting, falling
Find a balance, find a way
Is my center inside out? Or
Outside in? And who will say?

Where and what do I do next? And
Is there path or light ahead?
Take one step and then another
Live life living or as dead!

It is my choice! Not another's
That's the past! This is the now!
Lessons, teachers all around me
They will model, show me how

To live my life! Live it fully
All emotions—none left out
Teach me how to play with others
Clap, sing, dance, spin, run and shout!

Child within comes out to play now
Criticism—no! No more!
My best effort all that's needed
Self-applause? Yes! Hear me roar!

The beginning is the ending!
What was then, no longer true
The unknown remains a challenge
I can do it! So can you

Camus and Reiki

Camus arrives for Reiki now
He jumps into my lap
My hands his shoulders do embrace
And then he takes a nap

Jolie's not sure of energy
Her "treatment" is quite short
She tolerates some here and there
And leaves with grunt and snort

This energy is powerful
And packing quite a wallop
Burning new pathways straight with fire
Like wild horses gallop

Gently Offer Empathy

Understanding pain and sorrow
Gently offer empathy
Let another feel their feelings
Support and listen. Let them be

Who they are within this moment
Dragging past to present mind
Hard to grasp the depth of sorrow
Deaf with pain and often blind

This is grief and all evade it
Usually run away and hide
Doesn't work! Tide crests again and
Takes us on horrific ride

That circles over, under, back
Relentless in pursuit of soul
So armor up, prepare attack!
Reality will make us whole

Grief unresolved will bring us death
As systems fail and cancer spreads
Use honest facts and healing tears
Truth far surpasses fear and dread

As trauma oozes out of cells
And tissues tight with grief and pain
Life surges through heart, body, mind
And we claim joy in soul again

There are no easy paths for grief
Dissociated, far away
Come back to do your work for you
Then live and love another day

Most others will not understand
Your courage or your will to live
Your choice may cost you old time friends
But you've outgrown the gifts they give

They're trapped in patterns old and stale
It's fear that keeps them locked within
So grab your courage with both hands
And choose to thrive with joy to win!

I am Me

I was me before I met you
Hidden deep within. Inside
I want to show you who I am
Vulnerable. No foolish pride

Can't control how others see me
Thinking I am someone else
All my actions/thoughts aren't pretty
I am me and no one else

Some say I am wonderful and
Kind and loving, thoughtful too
Yes, I like to do for others
Also to receive from you

Don't need much to smile, be happy
Kindness, love, affection too
Respect for how I lived to get here
Problems overcome weren't few

Hard to find me under layers
Blocking bleeding from the past
Unclog filters deeply damaged
Free to breathe! See clear at last!

Some say leave the past behind you
Easier to say than do
Patterns old are hard to change
Create a vision clear and new

Specifically define what I
Am seeking, searching in the night
Step up to claim my turn, my time
Now or never! 'Tis my right

First required is forgiveness
For all of those who hurt me then
Forgive self too, and let all go
Remember—if not now, then when?

Anger, pain, a bitter burden
Blocks your access to the light
Always choose to start again
Choose happiness! Not being right

Being right is ever lonely
Deep within protective walls
Hard to see in mirror self
Desperation, illness calls

Since we're human, all make errors
Clean it up and start anew
Choose a path with smaller boulders
Always choice is up to you!

Carefully choose friends and choices
Consequences follow each
Pay attention. Listen hard
Know everything's within your reach

Need to know first what you want and
More than that to know the why
Of feelings roiling up within
That motivate to reach the sky

So reach out—grab the golden ring
When comes your turn to run the course
Run well. Your one and only chance
To drink life's cup direct from source

My Journey

Fall is drifting in the air now
Summer days are nearly gone
Soon the sky will fill with wings
Of birds who leave behind their song

Cooler days and colder nights
Presage the winter days to come
Now with quiet contemplation
We look to things as yet undone

Ran out of time for their completion
During summer's busy days
And still the tasks remain unfinished
In the setting sun's pale haze

Are the things we do important?
Or do they fill up time and space
Due to fear to seek within us
Stare in mirror? See a face?

Who is that who stares back at us?
Does she know her wants and needs?
Can she state them clear on paper?
Or is her garden full of weeds?

That have so long choked out her voice
It's now a whisper, not a shout
Does she know just what is missing?
Does she run away and pout?

Is it some other's job to do this?
Summer, Winter, Spring or Fall
Is it someone else's journey?
Does it matter? Is this all

There is to Life—this endless struggle?
Is this all that there will be?
There's another way to do this
A path that's easy, simple, free

Yes! It's called Belief in Self
One walks uneven, narrow path
Place one foot and then the other
Leave the crowd behind, the wrath

Of those who plunged o'er cliffs ahead
In their panicked raging dance
Wearing blinders as they run or
Never planning. Leave to chance

Things they do not want to do. They
Think in magic, fantasy
And they're surprised at the results
When all is said and done. You see

They ran away from Death. And
In so doing ran from Life
Skipped the things that needed doing
Supportive loving—husband, wife

They just stayed busy, busy, busy
Daytimes full from dawn to dark
At day's end they sat exhausted
Asking where they lost the spark

Of Joy in life they had as children
It got lost along the way
They don't make much time to find it
Way past time to learn to play

And the Seasons flowing softly
Echo down the passing years
Did I treasure each one's gifts or
Did I whine and fuss, cry tears?

Joy abundant with Acceptance
Summer, Winter, Spring or Fall
This is it! This is My Journey!
It's does matter! This is All!

2010

Relationships

What have I learned today of me?
I am not always what I see
Reflected in my bedroom glass
So many questions do I ask

Who's there behind the masks I wear?
A child of fear? Adult can't share?
Truth within the woman I see
Reflected in the mirror- me

I read alone. I'm quiet too
I really want to learn of you
The you behind the masks you share
The you when mask you do not wear

It's hard to put my fears aside
Replace delusions, pretense, pride
With true feelings, full disclosure
Replace armor with exposure

Of me, myself, just as I am
Can you accept without a plan
To change me into someone new
Who's not like me and more like you?

I need to know before we start
Before I share my loving heart
That you will not eradicate
The I that's me when we do mate

Two I's can soon become a we
Two you's, half-whole, need therapy
If I am whole and you are too
Then I'll stay me and you'll stay you

Acknowledgments

Many friends, teachers, and healers have been an essential part of my transformative journey, which is an ongoing process.

In 2020 I had a knee replacement. And in 2021 my health was impacted severely with a diagnosis of breast cancer resulting in a bilateral mastectomy.

I broke my left wrist in a fall in March 2022, cancer returned and seven more lymph nodes were removed in April. I fell and broke my right elbow during my time of twenty-five radiation treatments in May and June.

I was fully helpless and dependent on others, unable to write or cook or drive. Friends really showed up to help in so many ways with food or to drive me to appointments or just to cheer me up. There were many dark nights of the soul in that period, and I was unable to care for my dog Re'my.

And, of course, there has been the Covid pandemic and its devastating impact on us all. From that time on, my travels were cancelled and I lived like a hermit. My goal of visiting 200 countries almost vanished—it was interrupted at #181—Antarctica. Others are booked, but who knows what lies ahead? It is extremely stressful now to book trips and flights and get seats. I now book at least a day early and fly Business Class, as I tire very easily.

During this time I lost friends who could not comprehend what I was enduring and my adherence to the principles I had learned was sorely tested. With great difficulty I cut ties with these previously unrecognized co-dependents and the intensity and confusion of our relationships. I hope to be able to write about these episodes when my right hand is healed.

God's Will be done. I remain in gratitude for all He has given me, for my increasing clarity of vision, for finally practicing 'Less Is More' and for the following people who have greatly aided me in my journey. Without them there might not have been a journey.

— *Jennie Rose*

Healers:

*Special professionals who were
instrumental in my healing and recovery*

Lance Allen
Acupuncturist/healer and dearest friend

Dr. Loni Belyea
Physician, supporter

Maribeth Billings
Reflexologist/healer, driver, supporter

Debra Parker
Massage therapist/healer, friend

Dr. Sushma Patel and staff
Radiation Oncologist

Dr. Bailey Sanders
Surgeon

The Vein Clinic
Hillary, Leah, and Otis

Candace W.
Nurse to Dr. Belyea
Supporter, kind encourager

Greg Wilder
Rolfer/healer and dearest friend

Friends:

*Friends from previous trips
and times in my life who showed up
to be supportive and encouraging*

Jill Athby
Travel partner, good listener, friend

LeeAnn Carvalho
Friend, emails and supportive cards and calls

Ellie Collins
Driver, supporter, shopper, friend

Dr. Raul Cucalon
My friend from a trip to Cuba
who never failed to send a witty email
or supportive response to keep me going

Beverly DeGraas
Travel partner, friend, supporter,
cards and calls

Viola Denson
Army nurse friend, travel partner,
bedrock supporter with faith in me
for whatever and always

Quincy Garfield
Friend, supporter, encourager, book sender,
"my safe place to land"

Doris Gully
Friend, neighbor, driver, supporter, cook

Donna Hammond and Janet Stumps
My beloved family members
who sent hundreds of books to keep me sane

Vivian Harrington
Friend, driver, supporter, cook,
provider of beautiful cards and phone calls

Tina and Tony Jenkins
Great steaks and Key Lime Pies,
shoppers, battery fixers

Bonnie Johnson
Cook, organizer, supporter, friend, driver

Dr. W. Miller Johnstone and Staff
This Concierge group of kind and compassionate people really supports me and is there for me when the going gets rough. Thank you each so much

Cassie Lehr
Cook, counselor, nurse, driver,
supporter, friend

Joyce Lowry
Deep, dear friend for over 15 years,
Re'my's second mother

Cathy Maready and Kevin Nichols
Meatloaf magnificence to nurture me

Joy Meyer and Pat Mack
Travel friends and providing ongoing support
and reading poetry and sending love for years

Moore
Travel partner in Nepal, friend, supporter

Renata Mowry
Friend, neighbor, driver, supporter

Lillian Oldham
Cleaner of my house and organizer of my life,
friend, supporter

Pam Partis
Neighbor, friend, driver, supporter, shopper

Juan Quintana
My steadfast gardener and keeper of my sanctuary,
my friend and supporter

Karen Mireau Rimmer
Supporter, friend, publisher

Marian Snyder
Cousin, supporter, encourager, friend

**Southern Pines
United Methodist Church and Choir**
Prayers, cards, and food

Tommy Sweely
Pastor, visitor, and prayer leader for my wellness

Marie Turner
Episcopal church Secretary who gave me
support, flowers, calls, cards, a prayer cross,
a shawl, an angel, and put me on their prayer list

Mary Ann Welsch
Cook, supporter, shopper, friend, driver

Molly Wilson
Organizer, cook, supporter, friend, nurse

Resources

Addictions

Addicted to Shopping … and Other Issues Women Have with Money / Karen O'Connor

Anatomy of a Food Addiction: The Brain Chemistry of Overeating: An Effective Program to Overcome Compulsive Eating / Anne Katherine

Behind the 8-ball: A Guide for Families of Gamblers / Linda Berman and Mary-Ellen Siegel

Breaking Free from Emotional Eating / Geneen Roth

Drinking: A Love Story / Caroline Knapp

Eating Disorders: Obesity, Anorexia Nervosa, and the Person Within / Hilde Bruch, MD

The Golden Cage / Hilde Bruch, MD

Love Hunger: 10 Stage Life Plan for Your Body, Mind, and Soul / Frank Minirth, Paul Meier, Robert Hemfelt, Sharon Sneed, and Don Hawkins

The Owl Was a Baker's Daughter: Obesity, Anorexia Nervosa and the Repressed Feminine / Marion Woodman

PTSD and Addiction: A Practical Guide for Clinicians and Counselors / Jerry Boriskin

Perfect Daughters: Adult Daughters of Alcoholics / Robert J. Ackerman

The Secret Lives of Hoarders / Matt Paxton with Phaedra Hise

Stuff: Compulsive Hoarding and the Meaning of Things / Randy O. Frost and Gail Steketee

Adult Children

Adult Children of Abusive Parents: A Healing Program for Those Who Have Been Physically, Sexually, or Emotionally Abused / Steven Farmer
Adult Children: The Secrets of Dysfunctional Families / John Friel and Linda Friel
Adult Children as Husbands, Wives, and Lovers / Steven Farmer
Adult Children of Alcoholics / Janet Geringer Woititz
Affirmations for Adult Children of Abusive Parents / Steven Farmer
Daily Affirmations for Adult Children of Alcoholics / Rokelle Lerner
Grandchildren of Alcoholics: Another Generation of Co-Dependency / Ann W. Smith
Treatment of Adult Survivors of Childhood Abuse / Eliana Gil

Boundaries

Boundaries / Dr. Henry Cloud and Dr. John Townsend
Boundaries: Where You End and I Begin / Anne Katherine
Boundaries and Relationships / Charles L. Whitfield, M.D.
Where to Draw the Line / Anne Katherine

Boys/Finding Their Feminine

Battle for the Castle / Elizabeth Winthrop
The Castle in the Attic / Elizabeth Winthrop

Children

Please Stop Laughing At Us: One Survivor's Extraordinary Quest to Prevent School Bullying / Jodee Blanco

When Children Grieve: For Adults to Help Children Deal with Death, Divorce, Pet Loss, Moving, and Other Losses / John James and Russell Friedman, Leslie Landon Matthews

Codependence

Breaking Free: A Recovery Workbook for Facing Codependence / Pia Mellody and Andrea Wells Miller

Changing Course: Healing from Loss, Abandonment, and Fear / Claudia Black

Choices: Taking Control of Your Life and Making it Matter / Melody Beattie

Co-Dependence Misunderstood / Anne Wilson Schaef

Codependency Guide to the Twelve Steps: How to Find the Right Program for You and Apply Each of the Twelve Steps to Your Own Issues / Melody Beattie

Codependent No More: How to Stop Controlling Others and Manipulation of Dysfunctional Relationships / Pat Springle

The Disease to Please: Curing the People-Pleasing Syndrome / Harriet B. Braiker

Facing Codependence: What it is, Where it Comes From, How it Sabotages Our Lives / Pia Mellody

I'm Dying to Take Care of You: Nurses and Codependence, Breaking the Cycles / Candace Snow and David Willard

Love is a Choice: The Groundbreaking Book on Recovery for Codependent Relationships / Dr. Robert Hemfelt, Dr. Frank Minirth, Dr. Paul Meier

Love is a Choice (workbook): Dr. Robert Hemfelt,
    Dr. Frank Minirth, Dr. Paul Meier
Recovery from Rescuing / Jacqueline Castine
When I Say No, I Feel Guilty / Manual J. Smith

Communication / Listening

Kicking the Big But Syndrome / Eddie Conner
Listen Up: Hear What's Really Being Said:
    Improve Your Career
    and Your Life by Becoming a Better Listener / Jim Dugger

Emotions

Emotional Baggage (CD) / Claudia Black
Growing Yourself Back Up: Understanding Emotional
    Regression / John Lee
Putting the Past Behind You (CD) / Claudia Black
Unpacking Your Bags (CD) / Claudia Black

Grief

The Grief Recovery Handbook: The Action Program for
    Moving Beyond Death, Divorce, and Other Losses
    (20th anniversary edition) / John W. James and
    Russell Friedman
How to Survive the Loss of a Love / Melba Colgrove,
    Harold H. Bloomfield, and Peter McWilliams
Necessary Losses: The Loves, Illusions, Dependencies,
    And Impossible Expectations That All of Us Have to
    Give Up in Order to Grow / Judith Viorst

Life Skills / Guidance

9 Things You Simply Must Do To Succeed in Love and Life: A Psychologist Probes the Mystery of Why Some Lives Really Work and Others Don't / Dr. Henry Cloud

The Alchemist / Paulo Coelho

Everyday Grace: Having Hope, Finding Forgiveness, and Making Miracles / Marianne Williamson

Finding Your Way Home: A Soul Survivor Kit / Melody Beattie

Fire in the Soul: A New Psychology of Spiritual Optimism / Joan Borysenko

The Four Agreements: A Toltec Wisdom Book / Don Miguel Ruiz

Full Catastrophe Living: Using the Wisdom of Your Body And Mind to Face Stress, Pain, and Illness / Jon Kabat-Zinn

The Gifts of Imperfection: Let Go of Who You Think You're Supposed to Be and Embrace Who You Are: Your Guide to a Wholehearted Life / Brene Brown

Illuminata: A Return to Prayer / Marianne Williamson

Learned Optimism: How to Change Your Mind and Your Life / Martin E.P. Seligman

People of the Lie: The Hope for Healing Human Evil / M. Scott Peck, M.D.

The Power of Now / Eckhart Tolle

The Power of Your Other Hand: A Course in Channeling the Inner Wisdom of the Right Brain / Lucia Capacchione

The Road Less Traveled / M. Scott Peck, M.D.

Self Matters: Creating Your Life from the Inside Out / Phillip C. Mcgraw

The Three Boxes of Life and How to Get Out of Them:
An Introduction to Life/Work Planning /
Richard Bolles
What Color is Your Parachute?: A Practical Manual for
Job-Hunters and Career-Changers / Richard N. Bolles

Men's Issues

Angry Men and the Women Who Love Them:
Breaking the Cycle of Physical and Emotional Abuse /
Paul Hegstrom
Fire in the Belly: On Being a Man / Sam Keen
The Five Love Languages: Men's Edition /
Gary Chapman
The Flying Boy: Healing the Wounded Man /
John Lee He
I Don't Want to Talk About It: Overcoming the Secret
Legacy of Male Depression / Terrence Real
Living with the Passive Aggressive Man / Scott Wetzler
Man in the Mirror: Solving the 24 Problems Men Face /
Patrick Morley
The Peter Pan Syndrome / Dan Kiley
Understanding Masculine Psychology /
Robert A. Johnson
The Verbally Abusive Relationship: How to Recognize it
and How to Respond / Patrick Evans
The Wounded Male / Steven Farmer

Narcissism/Sociopathy

Confessions of a Sociopath: A Life Spent Hiding in Plain
Sight / M.E. Thomas
The Sociopath Next Door / Martha Stout

Will I Ever Be Good Enough?: Healing the Daughters of Narcissistic Mothers / Karyl McBride

The Wizard of Oz and Other Narcissists: Coping With The One-way Relationship In Work, Love, and Family / Eleanor D. Payson

Parents

Between Fathers & Daughters: Enriching and Rebuilding Your Adult Relationship / Linda Nielsen

Children of Fast-Track Parents: Raising Self-Sufficient And Confident Children in an Achievement-Oriented World /Andree Aelion Brooks

Don't Call Me Mother: Breaking the Chain of Mother-Daughter Abandonment / Linda Joy Myers

The Emotional Incest Syndrome: What to Do When a Parent's Love Rules Your Life / Dr. Patricia Love

Toxic Parents / Susan Forward

The Ultimate Betrayal: The Enabling Mother, Incest and Sexual Abuse / Audrey Ricker

The Wounded Woman: Healing the Father-Daughter Relationship / Linda Schierse Leonard

Relationships / Love Addiction

The Betrayal Bond: Breaking Free of Exploitive Relationships / Patrick Carnes

Controlling People: How to Recognize, Understand, and Deal with People Who Try to Control You / Patricia Evans

Facing Love Addiction: Giving Yourself the Power to Change the Way You Love / Pia Mellody

The Five Love Languages / Gary Chapman

The Five Love Languages of Apology / Gary Chapman

How to Break Your Addiction to a Person /
   Howard M. Halpern
The Intimacy Factor: The Ground Rules for Overcoming
   The Obstacles to Truth, Respect, and Lasting Love /
   Pia Mellody
The Intimacy Struggle: Revised and Expanded for All
   Adults / Janet G. Woititz
Intimate Partners: Patterns in Love and Marriage /
   Maggie Scarf
Is It Love or Is It Addiction? / Brenda Schaeffer
Love Smart: Find the One You Want –
   Fix the One You Got / Phil McGraw
Obsessive Love: When it Hurts Too Much to Let Go /
   Susan Forward and Craig Buck
Relationship Rescue: A Seven-step Strategy for Reconnecting with Your Partner / Phillip C. McGraw
We: Understanding the Psychology of Romantic Love /
   Robert A. Johnson
Women Who Love Too Much / Robin Norwood

Sex / Sex Addiction

Contrary to Love: Helping the Sexual Addict /
   Patrick Carnes
Don't Call it Love: Recovery From Sexual Addiction /
   Patrick Carnes
Lust, Anger, Love: Understanding Sexual Addiction and
   the Road to Healthy Intimacy / Maureen Canning
Out of the Shadows: Understanding Sexual Addiction /
   Patrick Carnes
Sexual Anorexia: Overcoming Sexual Self-hatred /
   Patrick Carnes
Sex & Power / Susan Estrich

Trauma, Recovery, Memory, Abuse

The Body Keeps the Score / Bessel Van der Kolk
The Body Never Lies: The Lingering Effects of Hurtful Parenting / Alice Miller
Breaking Down the Wall of Silence: The Liberating Experience of Facing Painful Truth / Alice Miller
The Drama of the Gifted Child: The Search for the True Self / Alice Miller
For Your Own Good: Hidden Cruelty in Child-rearing and the Roots of Violence / Alice Miller
From Rage to Courage: Answers to Reader's Letters / Alice Miller
Healing the Shame that Binds You / John Bradshaw
Healing from Trauma: A Survivor's Guide to Understanding Your Symptoms and Reclaiming Your Life / Jasmin Lee Cori
Healing Trauma: A Pioneering Program for Restoring the Wisdom of Your Body / Peter A. Levine
In an Unspoken Voice: How the Body Releases Trauma and Restores Goodness / Peter A. Levine
Memory and Abuse: Remembering and Healing the Effects of Trauma / Charles L. Whitfield
Paths of Life / Alice Miller
The Prince of Tides / Pat Conroy
Thou shalt Not Be Aware: Society's Betrayal of the Child / Alice Miller
Trauma and Recovery: The Aftermath of Violence from Domestic Abuse to Political Terror / Judith Herman
Traumatic Stress: The Effects of Overwhelming Experience on Mind, Body, and Society / Bessel A. Van der Kolk, Alexander C. McFarlane, and Lars Weisaeth

The Truth Will Set You Free: Overcoming Emotional Blindness and Finding Your True Adult Self / Alice Miller

The Untouched Key: Tracing Childhood Trauma in Creativity and Destructiveness / Alice Miller

Waking the Tiger: Healing Trauma / Peter A. Levine / Ann Frederick

Women's Books

Anatomy of the Spirit / Caroline Myss

The Cinderella Complex: Women's Hidden Fear of Independence / Collette Dowling

Conscious Femininity: Interviews with Marian Woodman / Marian Woodman

The Dance of Anger: A Woman's Guide to Changing the Patterns of Intimate Relationships / Harriet Lerner

The Dance of Connection: How to Talk to Someone When You're Mad, Hurt, Scared, Frustrated, Insulted, Betrayed, or Desperate / Harriet Lerner

The Dance of Deception: Pretending and Truth-telling in Women's Lives / Harriet Lerner

Dance of the Dissident Daughter: A Woman's Journey from the Feminine Face of God: The Unfolding of the Sacred in Christian Tradition to the Sacred Feminine / Sue Monk Kidd

In a Different Voice: Psychological Theory and Women's Development / Carol Gilligan

Meeting the Madwoman / Linda Schierse Leonard

Overcoming Perfectionism / Ann Smith

She: Understanding Feminine Psychology / Robert A. Johnson

The Silent Passage: Menopause / Gail Sheehy

Why People Don't Heal, How They Can / Caroline Myss

A Woman's Worth / Marianne Williamson
Women / Sherry Ruth Anderson and Patricia Hopkins
Women's Reality: An Emerging Female System in a White Male Society / Anne Wilson Schaef
Women Who Run with the Wolves: Myths and Stories of the Wild / Sacred Contracts: Awakening your Divine Potential Woman Archetype / Clarissa Pinkola Estes
The Wounded Woman / Linda Schierse Leonard

Jennie Rose

About the Author

Jennie Rose is a life and codependence counselor, with a focus on recovery from trauma.

After receiving her BSN from the University of Maryland on an Army scholarship, Jennie spent a total of twenty-seven years on active duty. Six of those years were as an Army-trained Pediatric Nurse Practitioner.

Jennie earned her MA from Webster University in 1981. As a Lieutenant Colonel in the U.S. Army Nurse Corps, she received her MEd at Boston University, European campus. It was there that her own journey towards healing from trauma began in 1987 with the help of "an enlightened witness."

Since then, Jennie has continued her intensive training in trauma therapy. It is her hope to offer to others the valuable pathway to peace and emotional wellness that she herself has been so fortunate to receive.

To Contact the Author
please email:
jrose109@nc.rr.com

To Contact the Publisher
please email:
Azalea.Art.Press@gmail.com

Direct Book Orders:
Lulu.com, Amazon.com, Barnes&Noble.com
and other online venues

www.ingramcontent.com/pod-product-compliance
Lightning Source LLC
Chambersburg PA
CBHW020350170426
43200CB00005B/124